below

Brooklyn
Is Not Expanding

Brooklyn
Is Not Expanding

Woody Allen's Comic Universe

Annette Wernblad

Rutherford ● Madison ● Teaneck
Fairleigh Dickinson University Press
London and Toronto: Associated University Presses

Associated University Presses
440 Forsgate Drive
Cranbury, NJ 08512

Associated University Presses
25 Sicilian Avenue
London WC1A 2QH, England

Associated University Presses
P.O. Box 39, Clarkson Pstl. Stn.
Mississauga, Ontario,
L5J 3X9 Canada

The paper used in this publication meets the requirements of the American National Standard for Permanence of Paper for Printed Library Materials Z39.48-1984.

Library of Congress Cataloging-in-Publication Data

Wernblad, Annette, 1958–
    Brooklyn is not expanding : Woody Allen's comic universe / Annette Wernblad.
        p.   cm.
    Filmography: p.
    Includes bibliographical references (p.   ) and index.
    ISBN 0-8386-3448-6 (alk. paper)
    1. Allen, Woody—Criticism and interpretation.   2. Comedy.
I. Title.
PN1998.3.A45W47   1992
791.43'092—dc20   90-56415
                                                                            CIP

To Allan

Contents

Preface

Woody Allen once said in a television interview:

> I always feel the burden of entertainment is on the filmmaker. And one great thing that the great filmmakers have, Bergman, Fellini, Bunuel, Truffaut, Antonioni, . . . they are all entertainers. . . . The audience has a right when they sit down to be entertained. No matter how intelligent your message is, no matter how smart or wonderful, progressive your ideas are, if they are not entertaining, then they should not be in a movie, you should write them in a journal.[1]

In the following pages I will examine Woody Allen's works, concentrating on the persona that he invented in his early days as a nightclub comedian and that forms the basis of his comic universe. I will trace the roots and follow the development of this character over the past decades as well as analyze its relevance for a sophisticated movie audience. It has been my intention to draw a sharp line between Woody Allen and his fictional creation. A number of critics have succumbed to the temptation of assuming that Woody Allen and his character are identical, that the opinions held by the Allen persona are also Woody Allen's personal opinions. My belief is that Allen, like any other artist, uses fragments of his personal experience in his work. That, however, does not necessarily indicate that his films are meant to be autobiographical.

I have to a great extent refrained from using biographical material in my analysis, partly because much of the existing material seems unreliable, and partly because Allen himself has repeatedly expressed a wish to remain anonymous—a wish that I think should be granted. But the main reason is that I feel that Allen's work is interesting enough in its own right.

Finally, in any analysis of Allen's work, it is vital to bear in mind that his central aim has always been to entertain. I have tried to write this book in that spirit, trying not to overanalyze lines that were meant purely as jokes. It is my sincere hope that my book has, as Richard Chase once said, "all the considerable advantages of being written by a sympathetic but critical foreigner."

Acknowledgments

My love and gratitude to my husband, Allan Poulsen, who is always willing to put everything on hold, for being such a wonderful cheering section and for making me laugh.

My warmest thanks to:
Richard Pells whose involvement in this project and faith in me from the very beginning has given me the courage and confidence to do more than I thought I could.

Edgar Doctorow, Thomas Elsaesser, and Sharon O'Brien for generously offering their help and encouragement at various stages of this book.

David Nye, Carl Pedersen, and Tonie Orvad Andersen, colleagues and friends, for giving me their time, support, and advice whenever I needed it.

My mother, who hates movies, for sitting through all of Woody Allen's films with me.

Tonny Pedersen for not spilling coffee on my manuscript and for always laughing at my jokes.

Finally, my appreciation to:
Lars Olgaard and the rest of the staff at the Danish Film Museum Library, Sidsel Brun at the Atheneum bookstore, the staff at the American Documentation Center in Copenhagen, and Hanne Drewsen and Marianne Charles at Nordisk Film.

At the beginning of *Radio Days,* Little Joe says that thanks to his Aunt Bea, he still gets "instant memory flashes" whenever he hears certain tunes. In addition to sometimes giving me an eerie feeling that he knows my most painful personal memories, Woody Allen has opened up a whole new universe of memories by means of his use of music. Thus I will never again be able to hear

Prokofiev's *Lieutenant Kije* without seeing Boris cavorting off with death. When I hear Harry James's *I've Heard That Song Before,* I immediately see Michael Caine running around in SoHo trying to "bump into" Barbara Hershey. I get these "instant memory flashes" whenever I hear *Rhapsody in Blue* or *South American Way* or *On a Slow Boat to China* or Louis Armstrong's recording of *Stardust* or Erik Satie's *Gymnopédies.* Since I started watching Allen's films, I must have bought a hundred new (or actually old) records. So to Woody Allen I would very much like to say, thank you for the memories!

Brooklyn
Is Not Expanding

1

A Shlemiel Is Born (1960–1969)

In every gang of kids spilling into the Jewish streets of 1900 or
1905—kids whose mothers hoped they would grow up to
become manufacturers, accountants, and doctors—there was
bound to be one who dreamed of "breaking in" with a comic
act or vaudeville troupe. It was a desire that often left him
uneasy: try explaining to immigrant parents that their darling
son wants to become a "bum" who cracks jokes in gentile
theatres.[1]

—Irving Howe

That their only son would grow up to become the world's leading
comic filmmaker, Nettie and Martin Konigsberg had never
dreamed, and if they had, they probably would not have liked the
idea. Allen Stewart Konigsberg was born in Flatbush, Brooklyn on
December 1, 1935, during the depression. He was apparently a
very introverted child who hated school and spent most of his free
time alone in his room practicing magic tricks or his clarinet. At
sixteen he started sending the best of the one-liners he thought up
to columists Walter Winchell and Earl Wilson under the name of
Woody Allen, and soon they started appearing in the papers.

His parents had a slightly different vision of their son's future.
As the children of Eastern European immigrants, they had spent
their early adult life trying to survive a depression. Consequently,
they had a powerful dread of poverty, and they wanted their son
to have the respectability and security of an education and a good
steady job, preferably in the fields of law or medicine. To please
them Allen entered New York University, but he was thrown out
after the first semester, and was thus able to devote his full
attention to writing jokes. By the time he was eighteen, he married
ex-fellow student, Harlene Rosen, and got a $175 a week job for
NBC as a writer.[2]

Today, four decades after his first jokes were published, Woody
Allen is a household name all over the world. He has written and

starred in dozens of movies, for himself as well as for other directors. He has published three books and had several plays successfully staged on Broadway and all over the United States and Europe. Yet, like his second generation predecessors whom Irving Howe is talking about in *World of Our Fathers*, he is "uneasy" about his parents. As he told one interviewer: "They would be much happier if I quit it all today and went to college and studied to be a pharmacist and went to work and made a hundred and twenty-five dollars a week for the rest of my life. With a pension. They have never been able to shake the feeling of imminent catastrophe. That's the way they grew up."[3]

In October of 1960, after several months of conning and urging, Allen's managers, Jack Rollins and Charles Joffe, succeeded in persuading him to perform his own material instead of merely writing jokes for other people, and landed him a job in Greenwich Village. However, despite his long and lucrative career as a writer, Woody Allen was not an instant success as a nightclub comic. Gradually he came to realize that despite the fact that he used the same type of jokes which had earned him his name as a writer, something was fundamentally wrong with his act: "I thought if S. J. Perelman went out and read, say, 'No Starch in the Dhoti, S'il Vous Plait,' they're going to howl. But that's not what it is at all; it's that the jokes become a vehicle for the person to display a personality. . . . I had it backwards. I was totally oriented as a writer."[4]

Accordingly, Woody Allen began molding a persona, and after two years of hard work, he managed to put together a truly professional act of highly integrated and interconnected jokes. His routines displayed a three-dimensional character, who had clearly inherited the feeling of "imminent catastrophe" from Allen's parents. So convincing was this character, whom Allen later used as a basis for his movies, that people tend to think that in private, as well as on the stage, Woody Allen *is* him. In one routine a neighborhood bully calls him "Red" because of the color of his hair. His reply is that his name is not "Red," but "Master Heywood Allen." In order not to confuse the private Woody Allen with his fictional creation, the latter will henceforth be referred to as Heywood Allen.

Heywood Allen is a peculiar looking fellow. He has thinning, red hair, a remarkably fair complexion, and a height considerably less than average. A pair of horn-rimmed glasses frame and dominate his face, and make him look rather like a walking apology for himself. His voice is high-pitched and squeaky, and when on stage he clings to the microphone as if afraid that he might fall. He is constantly cutting the air with his long, spindly arms; a gesture that makes him faintly resemble a fluttering insect. And his clothes—saddle shoes, suede jacket, and jeans— always (like the traditional clown's costume) seem slightly too big for him, thus emphasizing the pseudo-heroic content of his stories. Playing heavily on the feelings of pity which this insecure and painfully recognizable figure arouses in the audience, the two major topics of the routines are Heywood's unsuccessful love life and his peculiar tendency to appeal to the brutal traits in people with whom he associates.

One show opens by his informing the audience that he was forced to move into an expensive apartment on Fifth Avenue because he was "constantly getting mugged and assaulted" by neighborhood barbarians. Considering Heywood's pathetic exterior, aggression directed at him by "hairy knuckle types" with "vegetable mentality" is hardly surprising. Scarcely, however, has he moved into this new secure part of town before his doorman attacks him, and every now and then we find that in addition to various brutes, supposedly respectable people and institutions cannot resist attacking the dainty *nebbish*. When he is being beaten up in his lobby, the police take the side of the aggressor; when he forgets to return a book to the New York Public Library, his glasses are taken away for a year; and when, as a child, he goes to interfaith camp, he gets thrashed by "boys of all races and creeds." All the mechanical objects in New York—toasters, elevators, TV sets—seem to have formed a conspiracy against him. Even his parents resent him. When he gets kidnapped, they "snap into action immediately; they rent out my room."

His philandering has been equally traumatic. In one case his date gets arrested at the Stork Club by Israeli agents; in another, he removes his glasses in a hotel room and, stark blind, ends up making love to a mirror instead of the girl (probably the most extreme example of the Allen persona's narcissism). His ex-wife, "Quasimodo," would cook "Nazi recipes," and in philosophical discussions "prove that I didn't exist." He calls their marriage "The Oxbow Incident."

The majority of the ex-wife jokes, however, are directed at Heywood himself and not at the wife.[5] She is intellectually superior to him and always wins their arguments. When he calls her an immature woman, his explanation goes like this: "See if this is not immature to you. I would be home in the bathroom, taking a bath. And my wife would walk right in whenever she felt like and sink my boats." These jokes are, in fact, the traditional *Borscht Belt* wife and mother-in-law stories turned upside down: Heywood Allen is the one who is constantly nagging his wife, not the other way around. Ultimately the joke is on him.

Heywood Allen's stories about his family and Jewish acquaintances are mirror images of the jokes of the *Borscht Belt* comics and thus bear a great resemblance to those we find in the works of contemporary Jewish comics from Allan Sherman to Elaine May and Mike Nichols, and Mel Brooks's "2000 year old man." They could be compared even more illuminatingly to the novels of Philip Roth. Heywood's father, like the father figure in Roth's works, is a hard-working, self-sacrificing, unsuccessful, and slightly ridiculous person. Like Roth's characters from Alexander Portnoy to Nathan Zuckerman, Heywood Allen does not see his male parent as a model but feels a mixture of pity, guilt, and embarrassment about him. The poor insignificant man is fired and replaced by a "tiny gadget . . . that does everything my father does. Only it does it much better.—Depressing thing is my mother ran out and bought one."

His mother, likewise, is the Jewish martyr mother *in extremis*. When Heywood told her he was getting a divorce, she "put down her knitting. She got up. And went over to the furnace. And she opened the door. And she got in." Like Sophie Portnoy she brags to her friends about his accomplishments on the one hand, and constantly nags him about not living up to her expectations on the other. When he is thrown out of college, she locks herself in the bathroom and takes an overdose of Mah Jongg tiles.

Like Neil Klugman in Roth's *Goodbye, Columbus,* Heywood Allen has Jewish acquaintances that are ludicrously assimilated. The parents of one of his friends named their son Guy de Maupassant Rabinowitz ("Guy de," among friends), and in the 1940 Roosevelt/Dewey election [*sic*] they voted for Hitler. And Heywood's cousin has a wife who, like Brenda Patimkin, has had her nose lifted, but . . . "by a golf pro."

In spite of the similarities between Roth's novels and Woody Allen's stand-up routines, however, there is one crucial factor which dissociates the two, namely the central character himself. Though quite often he comes across as a *shlimazl,* the Heywood Allen persona is basically a *shlemiel.*[6]

In her *The Schlemiel as Modern Hero,* Ruth Wisse explains the difference thus:

> the *schlemiel* spills the soup, the *schlimazl* is the one into whose lap it falls. . . . The *schlemiel* is the active disseminator of bad luck, and the

schlimazl is its passive victim. . . . The *schlemiel*'s misfortune is his character. It is not accidental, but essential. Whereas comedy involving the
schlimazl tends to be situational, the *schlemiel*'s comedy is existential,
deriving from his very nature in its confrontation with reality.[7]

Even in the stories where Heywood Allen is the victim, this is
not "accidental" but very much part of his nature. When he tells us
that "I was once run over by a car with a flat tire being pushed by
two guys," the explanation of why this misfortune happened is
that "I have very bad reflexes." Although he is constantly being
victimized by everybody from his parents and his rabbi to neighborhood hooligans, Ernest Hemingway, and the New York Public
Library, his comedy is existential rather than situational.

Although Alexander Portnoy is called a *shlemiel* by an Israeli
woman (who uses the word invectively), he does not like this status
at all. In fact, the novel is an account of his unsuccessful attempt to
rid himself of the burden of his *shlemiel*hood. To understand his
attitude, one has to consider not merely the literal meaning of the
word *shlemiel* (loser), but also the long folklore tradition behind
the *shlemiel* figure.

He was "born" in the Russian and Eastern European *shtetl*
where his original function was, by means of his innocence and
simplicity, to point out the ludicrousness of his opponents. Instead of despairing over his impossible position and the frequent
pogroms, the *shlemiel* turned his weakness into strength by showing that morally he was in the right and his persecutors in the
wrong. The vocation, then, of this fictitious character was to
preserve sanity in himself, but certainly in his audience as well, in
an all but intolerable situation. His humor, as Wisse points out,
"contains more harshness than merriment."[8]

When Alexander Portnoy sees himself as the victim of a dirty
joke, and mocks the Jewish customs and attitudes still so paramount in his environment, it is because he considers these
customs as well as the *shlemiel* figure unnecessary in the liberated
American 1960s. Although religious rituals and an exaggerated
sense of humor based on one's own weakness may have been
necessary to survive in the *shtetl*, they are, in Portnoy's eyes, super-
fluous and ridiculous in the New World.

Woody Allens's use of the *shlemiel* figure on the other hand
seems both relevant and capable of drawing a vast amount of
recognition and identification from a contemporary audience.
This is primarily because his emphasis is rather different from
that of the folklore tales. Originally the *shlemiel* was used as a

means of preserving sanity in the *shtetl* community; the Heywood Allen figure is used to do so in contemporary Western society. The implication of Allen's routines is that in an environment where Park Avenue doormen and the New York City police cannot be trusted, the born loser may be the only morally sane man. In modern America, pogroms and intolerable living conditions for the Jews have very little relevance. And what Heywood Allen is up against is indeed not so much anti-Semitism as the inherent values of a twentieth-century setting and the standards that modern man, as defined by *Playboy* magazine, is supposed to aspire to. As Heywood's physical appearance suggests before he even starts talking, he is not capable of living up to very high norms regarding libidinousness, and it is thus necessary for him to deflate his enemies instead.

If the effect that the Allen persona achieves by showing the ludicrousness of his opponents is that of the Yiddish *shlemiel,* the means he uses to deflate them stems from quite another comic tradition, namely that of the con man. While the *shlemiel* tradition is rural and Eastern European, the con man, like Allen himself, has his roots in urban America. What characterizes the con man is his snottiness. When he is at a physical, social, or intellectual disadvantage, the con man ridicules his adversary by means of oral ingenuity and rapidity (usually behind their backs). His victories are in fact almost always verbal. Thus Heywood Allen, in the spirit of his predecessors, Groucho Marx, W. C. Fields, and Bob Hope, calls the boyfriend of one of his dates a "post-impressionist, mock, pseudo, psychotic, neo-quasi, cretin painter." His intellectual, ultra-hip beatnik friends and aquaintances—a category of people whose self-opinionated, drug-oriented peer group pressure Allen disdainfully debunks in the stand-up routines as well as in his movies—write theses on topics like "The Increasing Incidents of Heterosexuality Amongst Homosexuals," and spend their evenings listening to "Marcel Marceau records."

The anxieties that Heywood Allen experiences are well known to a contemporary audience: the fear of not living up to the sexual and intellectual expectations of our peers, and the alienation one feels in a modern, mechanized society, where machines and bureaucracies do not always function quite the way one would like them to. Audiences thus readily identify with Allen's *shlemiel* and rejoice in his verbal victories. To emphasize this sense of identification even further, Allen universalizes the traditional Yiddish figure. In one of the routines, Heywood tells us of a script he wrote for a science fiction film. The plot goes as follows: one afternoon the whole world "mysteriously falls asleep," and the humans, when they wake up an hour later, find that they are all "in the pants business." A spaceship full of extraterrestrials come down, and the entire human race, now in the stereotypically Jewish tailor profession, is compelled to sew pants and do dirty laundry for the space men. Having been humiliated thus, the human beings, like the traditional *shlemiel,* get the last laugh over their oppressors. The extraterrestrials "are foiled, 'cause they travel 117 million light years to pick . . . up [the laundry] and they forget their ticket."

Taking the step from identifying with Heywood Allen toward concluding that he is identical with Woody Allen—the way a number of critics and fans have—is nevertheless a gross misconception. Allen is a serious and un-bungling person whose greatest concern in life seems to be not his degree of success with the opposite sex, but his work, toward which he has a very professional attitude. "I never get so depressed that it interferes with my work," he once told an interviewer. "I'm disciplined. I can go into a room every morning and churn it out."[9] Editor Ralph Rosenblum, who worked closely with Woody Allen for nearly a decade (from *Take the Money and Run* [1969] to *Interiors* [1978]), accurately describes how Allen dissociates from his figure: "The insecurity and fears are truly his own, but the behavior is not. He is not a bumbler. He is not ingratiating. He rarely makes an effort to be affable to strangers."[10]

There are several understandable explanations as to why the public assumes that Allen and his *shlemiel* are identical. One is the fact that the comic, because of the audiences' identification with him, often is expected to be funny even in private. Whereas nobody supposes that Marlon Brando behaves like Stanley Kowalski or Robert De Niro like Travis Bickle, most of us probably believe that Groucho Marx bore a constant resemblance to Rufus T. Firefly and feel a little cheated over Chaplin's invention of a hostile and unfunny character like Monsieur Verdoux. Another explanation could be the fact that when an actor is seen repeatedly in the same kind of role, as is often the case with comedians, we tend to identify him with the type he portrays in private as well as on the screen.

More important, however, is the fact that Woody Allen in his routines keeps leading us on to believe that the *shlemiel* persona really is himself. He opens one show: "Since I was here last, a lot of significant things have occured in my private life that I thought we could go over tonight," and around the middle of the show he insists once again that "these stories are true. These things actually happen to me." The name he uses for his figure is practically his own—except, of course, Woody Allen is not his real name. He even uses incidents that the audience knows to have happened in his private life, such as his having been married twice, sued by his ex-wife, and gone to Europe to film *What's New, Pussycat?*

These events, though, are not presented altogether truthfully, which suggests that perhaps their assumed autobiographical content should not be taken too seriously. One obvious example would be Heywood's description of his first meeting with his second wife: "I go to a four floor walk-up. And I knock on the door. And this girl comes to the door. And she's absolutely beautiful. But really terrific. Great long, blond hair, a short skirt, and boots, and a sleeveless jersey, and she's packed into it." This woman, although undoubtedly a knock-out, has absolutely nothing in common with Woody Allen's second wife, Louise Lasser.

In interviews Allen likewise does his best to make us believe that his persona is all but indistinguishable from himself. A closer look, however, reveals that most of what he "confides" in interviewers about his private fears and failures is strictly fictitious. In fact, there are a number of examples where Allen clearly—much like his *shlemiel*—turns the tables on nosy, but credulous reporters who are trying to enter his private domain.[11]

According to Ralph Rosenblum, he and Woody Allen have a lot of traits in common: "We are both . . . perennially joyless, pessimistic about our chances for happiness, and easily sucked into low spirits." The two of them worked together on a very close professional basis for nearly ten years, yet, Rosenblum says, "we've never shared a heartfelt concern, an uninhibited laugh, an open display of anger."[12] To assume, then, although admittedly it can be very tempting, that Woody Allen would confide in an audience or an interviewer, is finally presumptuous and naive. Although at times his paranoid New Yorker mannerisms may seem strange even to his close friends, Woody Allen is not a *shlemiel,* not a bungler, and not Heywood Allen. Already in his early routines do we glimpse an enormously professional talent. His stories are constructed so that, rather than being merely jokes piled upon jokes, they are tightly integrated. Like a snowball running down a mountain they have what Henri Bergson called "an effect which grows by arithmetical progression, so that the cause, insignificant at the outset, culminates by a necessary evolution."[13]

One routine which precisely illustrates the aptness of applying

Bergson's theory to Allen's work is the story of the "Deep South" costume party. It shows Heywood Allen's roots in the *shlemiel* and con man traditions in that ultimately he manages to turn the tables on his opponents. It presents him as the native New Yorker who, try as he may, cannot escape his urbanity and his Jewishness, and finally it discloses him as a dreamer whose tendency to slip into wild Hollywood-tinted fantasies and misrepresentations of reality we shall take a closer look at in the following chapter.

In this particular story, Heywood tells us that once, when he was "down South," he was invited to a costume party. At first he did not want to go, but then he said to himself: " 'What the hell, it's Halloween, I'll go as a ghost.' So I take the sheet off the bed and throw it over my head, and I go to the party. And you have to get the picture. I'm walking the street in a Deep Southern town, I have a white sheet over my head. A car pulls up and three guys with white sheets say, 'Get in!' So I figure they're guys going to the party—as ghosts, and I get into the car."

Eventually poor Heywood realizes that "I'm sitting there between four klansmen. Four big-arm men. And the door is locked. And I'm petrified." He tries to hide his identity by constantly saying "you all" and "grits." Eventually he gives himself away, " 'cause they asked for a donation and everybody there gave cash. When it came to me I said, 'I pledge $50.' " The klansmen decide to hang the imposter, and suddenly, Heywood tells us, "my whole like passed before my eyes: I saw myself as a kid again. Kansas, goin' to school, swimmin' at the swimmin' hole. Fishin'. Fryin' up a mess o' catfish. Goin' down to the general store, gettin' a piece of gingham for Emmy Lou. And I realize it's not my life. They're going to hang me in two minutes, the wrong life is passing before me." Heywood panics and frantically gives a "really eloquent" speech about how the country can only survive if we all love each other "regardless of race, creed or color." He manages not only to persuade the klansmen to cut him down and let him go, but also to sell them $2,000 worth of Israel bonds.

Just as the traditional function of the *shlemiel* was to heighten the sense of survival in its audience, so Woody Allen's persona is himself a survivor. In the "Deep South" routine, Heywood Allen illustrates his ability to outsmart not only the Ku Klux Klan, but the Grim Reaper as well. Many of Allen's subsequent characters in his movies and short essays are survivors like Heywood, and Allen's humor, like the *shlemiel*'s, has a very fundamental survivor's instinct behind it. One potent way of illustrating this instinct would be to juxtapose Allen's stand-up routines with those of Lenny Bruce, the one of Allen's contemporaries whom he least resembles.

The Allen persona, as we have seen, offends and deflates the people he does not like, and his verbal triumphs and revenge are transferred to the audience in the form of relief. Bruce, in contrast, who is all but indistinguishable from his stage persona, ridicules even the people with whom he sympathizes and identifies, and consequently he offends and deflates himself. His "enemies" are not very clearly defined, and thus he mocks women, feminists, and lesbians as well as male-chauvinists, Jews as well as anti-Semites, blacks as well as racists, and—toward the end of his career—the legal system that kept dragging him in and out of court as well as his own inability to cope. What is transferred to *his* audience is not relief, but Bruce's frantic and absurd sound and fury, signifying less and less. Where Allen's humor is basically a survivor's humor, Bruce's (to quote himself) "is based on destruction and despair. If the whole world were tranquil, without disease and despair, I'd be standing in the breadline right back of J. Edgar Hoover."[14]

There are a number of topics that both comics deal with in which the difference is palpable. In his Jewish jokes, Allen is relatively good humored. He mocks his rabbi because when he was on TV he could not think of the Ten Commandments and named the seven dwarfs instead. Bruce's Jewish routines are not so harmless:

> Now the Jews celebrate this holiday, Rose-o-shonah and Yom-ky-poor, where they, actually, they celebrate the killing of Christ. Underground. You know, when they all get loaded, and, you know, they just: "Oh ho ho! We killed him! Ho ho! More chicken soup! Oh ho ho ho!" You know, kids running around with wooden sticks in the back-yard: "C'mon! Come up the hill. Come up the hill to Gethsemane." You know.

Similarly, the emphasis in Allen's sex jokes is on Heywood's own shortcomings and failures, whereas Bruce's are savage and malicious. One instance would be his long and painful dialogue between a bus driver and Paul Newman when the latter exposes himself on a bus:

> *Bus driver:* Mr. Newman, you've got your joint out!
> *Newman:* I can't come any other way! Hehehehe!

Finally, the Allen *shlemiel,* as we have seen, treats death as a subject to be dealt with mockingly, while Lenny Bruce's stage persona is morbidly obsessed with it. Based on Elisabeth Kübler-Ross' theories, Bruce divides the process of death into five stages and acts out each stage: "Anger, Denial, Bargaining, Depression, and Acceptance! Sounds like a Jewish law firm."[15]

On a completely unsubtle level, of course, Allen's and Bruce's respective forms of comedy are reflected in their lives with Allen's success and Lenny Bruce's premature death. Allen is a survivor in less literal ways as well, though. Just as Hollywood was severely crippled by the advent of television in the late 1940s and early 1950s, so the world of stand-up comedy felt the effect of its increasing power approximately a decade later. Instead of going out to theaters and clubs once or twice a week, people—an even larger percentage of whom had now moved from the city to the suburbs—stayed home to watch TV. Whereas Hollywood reacted to the new medium by transforming itself and offering epics that television, because of its standard ratio could not imitate, the stand-up comedians did not seem to reevaluate their own art form but merely to consider whether to "sell out" and work within television, or go on as if nothing had happened.

For many of Allen's contemporaries working within the tepid, commercial medium of television was a compromise they were not willing to make, but for quite a few others there was not even a choice. People like Lenny Bruce and Mort Sahl were politically oriented comics who were liable to offend the values of the average American viewer with their controversial opinions, and thus they were "not suited" for television. Allen's routines on the other hand are purposefully unpolitical. As he said himself: "I've always tried not to be a topical satirist because it dates so quickly. You can get cheap laughs making Nixon jokes and it seems like you're saying something, too, but five years later the stuff will be dead as can be. I like a broader kind of humor, one that's less calculated."[16]

Thus Allen, with his less offensive material, was more generally acceptable on national television, and of course he knew the medium from his days as a writer there. Unlike many of his colleagues, he survived the transition relatively painlessly. Even he, however, had no intention of staying in the world of television forever. For him, as for his contemporaries, working there was a slightly immoral compromise. Yet he was willing to make that compromise in order to gain experience and recognition so that— like Elaine May and Mike Nichols—he would be able to pit himself against yet another medium, film, as was his real ambition. When working on television, he told one critic, he felt like "a Renaissance painter who worked on sand. You have to pick a medium that has some staying power. Stage is fun but if you're trying to accumulate a body of work with substance to it, you need film."[17]

One evening in 1964, Woody Allen's wish was granted: producer Charles Feldman saw him perform in the *Blue Angel* in Greenwich Village, and through Allen's managers, Jack Rollins and Charles Joffe, "purchased" him to write the screenplay for a film, *What's New, Pussycat?* Unfortunately, working for Feldman turned out to be not very different from working for television. Allen later described the project as "terribly unsatisfying, a compromise."[18]

The supposedly comic basis of the movie is the constellation of sex-hungering losers, Victor Shakapopolis and Fritz Fassbender, with compulsive Casanova, Michael James. Where Michael constantly "scores" much to his—and his fiancée's—regret, Fritz and Victor never do, much to theirs. Because Feldman wanted the movie to center on Michael James, Allen had to constantly change his script, which predictably showed a much greater understanding for the "bunglers." Although its few genuinely funny scenes clearly stem from his pen, the finished product has very little to do with Woody Allen. His persona was superficially transferred to the screen with no form of visual development, and Victor Shakapopolis is a *shlemiel* only in the most basic meaning of the word, namely a loser.[19]

What's New, Pussycat? is an embarrassingly unfunny film, whose male and female characters alike are unconvincing stereotypes. Its sex-crazy plot, which may have been regarded as "hip" in the mid-sixties, seems from a 1990s point of view pathetically bawdy.[20] With its impressive international cast, however, it was a tremendous box-office success, so that along with the other Feldman movie Woody Allen was in, *Casino Royale* (where his persona has the exact same function of sex-hungering loser), he could use it as a stepping stone to further his career.

Allen has disowned the two Feldman movies in public, regarding *What's New Pussycat?* as a compromise and *Casino Royale* as "an unredeemingly moronic enterprise from beginning to end."[21] His own first cinematic project, *What's Up, Tiger Lily?* suffered the same fate: "I hated *What's Up, Tiger Lily?* and sued to keep it from coming out."[22] *Tiger Lily* is a Japanese James Bond spoof (whose new title obviously echoes *Pussycat*), which Allen and a few of his friends were to re-edit and provide with a new humorous soundtrack.

Although it is no masterpiece, *Tiger Lily* is infinitely more original than either Feldman project, and in its plot structure and breaking of cinematic conventions, it anticipates some of Woody Allen's very best works. The idea of adding an asynchronous, humorous soundtrack is developed in several of the later movies, as is the split screen technique. Toward the end of the film, Allen himself is lying on a couch on the left side of the screen while an Oriental lady is stripping on the right side. The camera pans to the right until Allen is excluded, and the stripper continues on the left side of the screen. On the right side we now see the conventional statement about the film being entirely fictitious. Immediately afterward another statement follows: "If you have been reading this instead of looking at the girl, then see your psychiatrist, or go to a good eye doctor." After which follows an eye chart.

For the first time in Allen's film career, no limitations are forced upon his own humor, and thus many of the jokes are familiar variations of his stand-up routines. The Oriental hero of the film is named Phil Moskowitz, and the plot is pervaded with Yiddish jokes. Says one character about the villains "They kill, they maim, and they even call up Information for numbers they could easily look up in the book." In spite of Woody Allen's personal dislike of his first venture, it is in that film and not the Feldman productions that the career of the most gifted of our contemporary comic film directors began.[23]

Despite all his frustrations, Allen did have a number of other more satisfying schemes revolving in the period from 1965 to 1967. He started writing short humorous essays for the *New Yorker* (which were collected in *Getting Even* in 1971); on February 2, 1966, he married Louise Lasser; and on November 17, 1966, his first play, *Don't Drink the Water!* opened at the Morosco Theatre in New York.

The play takes place in a United States Embassy in an unnamed Iron Curtain country, where a vacationing New Jersey caterer, Walter Hollander, and his family take refuge when they are accused of espionage by the local Communist goverment. Because Ambassador Magee is out of the country, the embassy is temporarily run by his blundering son, Axel, with the help of the efficient "punctilious rat," Kilroy. Within a few hours, by the joint efforts of Axel Magee and the Hollanders, to Kilroy's great dismay the embassy is a madhouse. This is the situation around which the comedy of the play evolves.

Don't Drink the Water! is one of the extremely few works in the first two decades of Allen's career which is not centered around the Allen persona. There are, however, elements of him in several of the characters. The character who resembles the Allen figure on the most immediate level—and whom he probably would have played had he not been in London filming *Casino Royale*—is Axel Magee. Like the *shlemiel,* Axel is too honest and innocent to understand politics. Unlike him, however, Axel does not make his opponents look ridiculous. He is merely a dunce whose life has been "like the Old Testament. The only thing I've been able to avoid so far is locusts." He is a victim who has a "vast experience getting stoned and spit at," and when he was naughty as a child, his mother would hit him with a copy of *Time* magazine with his father's photo on the cover. He is, in fact, closer to the *shlimazl* than the *shlemiel* in that he is the one into whose lap the soup constantly falls.

The second character who calls to mind the stand-up persona is Father Drobney, who is probably inspired by the Cardinal Mindzenty case. Like the Hollanders, Father Drobney is a refugee from the Communist police, and he has been hiding in the embassy for six years. He functions as the narrator of the play who opens and closes it, and on several occasions breaks out from the plot to speak directly to the audience. He is the character who—like Heywood Allen—establishes contact with the audience so that rather than being mere spectators, they are consulted and involved. We shall meet narrator figures in different shapes all through Allen's work.

Another trait in many of Allen's later characters, which we first see in Father Drobney, is an interest in magic. To pass "the lonely moments" of his captivity, he has invented a hobby for himself: performing magic tricks. In her book ". . . *but we need the eggs,*" Diane Jacobs bases her entire interpretation of Allen's works on her theory that in them there is a conflict between "reality—or life as it is—and magic—or life as one's mind and imagination can transform it."[24] She sees Allen's characters as solidly rooted in a dull reality which they are trying nobly to transcend by means of their imagination.

We do indeed find a fundamental conflict between magic and reality in most of Allen's works. But although Allen's persona—at least initially—sees his dreams as preferable to reality, it is a misconception to assume that Allen himself shares this view (again we see the tendency to confuse Allen with his *shlemiel*). In fact, Allen's moral—and he *is* a moralist—is usually the very opposite of what Jacobs suggests. Thus, Father Drobney, like most of the other "magicians" in Allen's work, is a failure; his magic does *not* work. Likewise the comic basis of many of Allen's other characters is that they are so absorbed in and blinded by their fantasies that they cannot distinguish between dream and reality and are incapable of living a dignified life. (Examples of this type of character would be Allan Felix of *Play It Again, Sam!*, Virgil Starkwell of *Take the Money and Run!*, and Professor Sidney Kugelmass of the short story "The Kugelmass Episode," who—as we shall see in chapter 5—is literally trapped in his fantasy.) Like Heywood Allen these characters keep slipping into Hollywood inspired daydreams that are no less demeaning than their everyday lives.

A number of other characters in Allen's works are so conventional and inflexible that for them there is only *one* reality, namely *their* everyday lives, of which they are extremely proud. Thus, they are incapable of reacting to abnormal situations, which, after all, are as much a part of reality as anything else. (One of the best examples of this type of character is the bank teller in *Take the Money and Run!*, who is so preoccupied with trying to find out if Virgil has misspelled his note that he does not realize that the bank is being robbed.)

Walter and Marion Hollander definitely belong in this second category. They are trapped in an embassy in Eastern Europe, surrounded by searchlights and professional killers with machine guns, yet they go on living their "normal" lives as if they were still in New Jersey. Marion starts cleaning the embassy, waxing the floors, and doing everybody's laundry. Walter frets about his catering business and about his and Marion's teenage son who is at summer camp back in the States: "Camp ends tomorrow. If we're not back to let him in, what's going to happen? He'll be unsupervised. He'll live in the streets. He'll run amuck. He'll rape and loot." Walter's worries in the embassy likewise have to do not with the bombs that are flying through the windows, but with everyday trivialities such as the menu and his having to sleep on a cot. Both Walter and Marion see and hear only what they want to see and hear, and thus only know the part of reality that they find pleasant. Every time somebody says something they do not want to know, they cover their ears and start singing *A Foggy Day in London Town*.

Ironically enough, however, Walter Hollander is the third character who represents a side of the Allen persona: the snotty combatant against pomposity and moral corruption.[25] He never passes a chance to deflate the many complacent characters in the play, among them the chef, the head of the Communist police, and the powerful Sultan of Bashir whom he calls "Aladdin" and "Fatso." He criticizes the violent politics of the latter, and in the true spirit of the Allen persona says, "I always read things in the papers and I get frustrated because being a little shot from New Jersey I never get a chance to express my opinion to a real big shot."

Although it was an audience success, the play got very mixed reviews when it first opened. Critics complained about its "exhausting excess of unmotivated one-liners."[26] One should keep in mind though that Woody Allen, in a 1966 interview, emphasized that what he wanted with the play was not to "write anything deep; I want to amuse people and please them while they're in the theatre."[27] Allen succeeded in doing just that. For all its "unmotivated one-liners," most of which by the way are hilarious, *Don't Drink the Water!* is a more than competent first try for a young comic playwright. In its most vigorous scenes, the play comes close to being as anarchicly funny as George S. Kaufman at his best. And there is an almost Groucho Marx-like insolence about Walter Hollander's insults. The most inspired scene is the one where chaos finally triumphs over order. Kilroy, who is the only stable ingredient in the play, gets hit in the head by a flying brick and deliriously thinks that he is the Wright brothers:[28]

> Come quickly, Wilbur. I'm coming, Orville. I'm telling you, Wilbur, we can do it. Do what? Get those machines to fly. Orville you're crazy. But so are you. Let's go down to Kitty Hawk Friday and put it in the air.— Wilbur, we must try it and stop arguing. Orville, you always were mother's favorite.

In 1969, *Don't Drink the Water!* was turned into a movie, which, although not nearly as lively and considerably more sterile than the play, is a relatively faithful adaptation. There is a slight change of emphasis, however. First of all, the Jewish Hollanders (who originally were played by Lou Jacobi and Kay Medford) are turned into WASPs and played by Jackie Gleason and Estelle Parsons. Furthermore where the entire play takes place in the embassy building, showing its quiet elegance before the arrival of the Hollanders, the movie almost artificially makes use of its possibilities for changing the geographical setting. It opens in Newark, New Jersey, showing us the Hollanders in their familiar surroundings before their disastrous vacation. In the play the Hollanders are seen as the disruptive force whose presence wrecks the embassy. In the film, in their "WASP'ness" they come across as relatively more harmless. After all their New Jersey home was not all that chaotic. The disruptive force is thus, by implication, their new setting: the Eastern European country which has now been named "Vulgaria."

Finally, the ending is changed slightly. In the play Father Drobney tells us how the Hollanders escaped; in the movie version, where he does not function as narrator, he—incredibly—escapes with them. In the play, the magician could not escape his reality; in the film, he does. In the next chapter we shall see a character for whom the reverse liberation takes place—a character who finally manages to escape his dream.

2

Here's Looking at You, Kid! (1969–1971)

> He filled his mind with all that he read . . . with enchantments,
> quarrels, battles, challenges, wounds, wooings, loves, torments
> and other impossible nonsense; and so deeply did he steep his
> imagination in the belief that all the fanciful stuff he read was
> true, that to his mind no history in the world was more authen-
> tic.[1]
>
> —Miguel de Cervantes, *Don Quixote*

As soon as he had finished his work on *Casino Royale* in 1967,
Woody Allen started working on two new projects, both of which
were released in 1969: a movie over which he had complete
control as a writer, director, and actor, and another play, this time
starring himself. The title of the play, *Play It Again, Sam!* refers—
naturally—to the famous line that Humphrey Bogart never actually spoke in *Casablanca*. Its central character, Allan Felix, is a
movie fanatic who tries to invoke and emulate his great hero,
Bogart, in an attempt to get over his recent divorce. Allan Felix is
the first—and probably best—example of the aforementioned
type of Allen persona who, rather than simply trying to escape an
unpleasant reality by daydreaming, is so caught up in his fantasy
that he believes it to be reality. In the process, he comes across not
as the Don Juan he aspires to, but rather as a modern day Don
Quixote.

Play It Again, Sam! is constructed in a nonlinear fashion which is
much more conventional in cinema than in drama (one reason
why the play seems more original than the film based on it). The
play is divided into scenes presenting an outer reality—what actually happens in Allan Felix's life—and scenes presenting an inner
reality—Allan's memories of and conversations with his wife
Nancy, his wild reveries about seducing "dames," and his con-
sultations with Humphrey Bogart on how to go about resuscitat-
ing his nonexistent love life.

The two other central characters in the play are Allan's best friend, Dick Christie, and Dick's wife, Linda. Dick is a very ambitious young businessman, and the great realist of the play (whose view of reality, incidentally, is as flexible as Walter Hollander's). When Allan tells them that Nancy left him, Dick says to Linda, who is devastated: "Why do you feel like crying? A man makes an investment—it doesn't pay off." A bond between Allan and Linda is established from the very beginning. They both want to love and be loved as intensely and irrationally as Vincent van Gogh who cut off his ear for a woman, and they have a wonderful time discussing their mutual neuroses and inferiority complexes.

All through the rest of the play, Dick and Linda try to find a suitable girl for Allan. Unfortunately he fails miserably with every date they get him because—emulating his macho hero—he insists on trying to act out his dreams of Hollywood romance. Linda keeps urging Allan to give up his phoney facade: "You don't need an image, be yourself. The girl will fall in love with you." But the only woman Allan is capable of acting naturally with is Linda herself. Eventually Linda—who is greatly neglected by her husband—fulfills her own prophesy: she falls in love with Allan and he with her.

Finally, at the end of the play, all three characters come to their senses. Dick realizes that he is losing Linda and should pay more attention, Linda decides that she does not want to give up her marriage, and Allan sees that ultimately his macho impersonations were precisely what antagonized his dates. Dick is off to Cleveland, and Linda and Allan follow him to the airport to clear up the situation. Allan urges Linda to go with her husband and bids her goodbye with Rick Blaine's speech to Ilsa from the last scene of *Casablanca*—an opportunity for which he has been waiting all his life: "If that plane leaves the ground and you're not with him, you'll regret it.—Maybe not today, maybe not tomorrow, but soon and for the rest of your life." Finally Bogart himself takes leave of Allan, saying, "You don't need me anymore. There's nothing I could show you you don't already know."

The play ends when Barbara Tyler, who has just moved in upstairs, comes down to use Allan's phone. She turns out to be a film buff and an admirer of Allan's articles in *Film Quarterly*. The rest is left to our imagination.

In the 1972 film version of *Play It Again, Sam!*, the last scene has been removed. After Bogart leaves him, and Dick and Linda go off to Cleveland together, Allan Felix is alone at the airport. The intention of this ending is more or less the same as that of the play.

Allan has come *down* to reality, as it were, and realized that trying to transcend it by dreaming is ridiculous as well as a hindrance to living a real life. In the play, his progress is substantiated and rewarded in the scene with Barbara. In the last scene of the film, which is in some ways more effective, his newfound "maturiosity" is its own reward. He is capable not only of being himself, but of being by himself. For Allan Felix, having a "mate" is not a "must" anymore, the way it is in Dooley Wilson's song from *Casablanca*.

In a number of accounts of Allen's work, his persona is described as a hopelessly incompetent and ugly loser, who desperately wants but cannot get hold of ample-bosomed women. Whereas this view of him is generally accepted among Allen's audience as well as his critics, it is misconceived in more ways than one. First, the *shlemiel* character is not merely a loser but has a much more complex function as we saw in the previous chapter. Second, only in the Feldman films and *Play It Again, Sam!* does the Allen figure frantically pursue unattainable women. These films have, no doubt, had a considerable influence in establishing the image of the lascivious loser, but, nevertheless, the Allen persona in his subsequent films has no trouble finding sex partners and seems more interested in the hopeless task of creating a lasting relationship with the woman he is in love with than with getting laid. Thus in *Bananas* Fielding has absolutely no trouble getting the oversexed revolutionary Yolanda into bed. What he does have problems with is his serious relationship with the not so fantastic Nancy as happens similarly in *Love and Death* with the Countess Alexandrovna and Sonia respectively. In the later films such as *Annie Hall, Manhattan,* and *Stardust Memories,* the persona's problem is not meeting women but rather holding on to meaningful relationships.

On the basis of this impression of the persona as a frantic pursuer of beautiful women, Allen has often been accused by critics (most notably Vivian Gornick) of male chauvinism. This charge, it would seem, reveals not only a poor sense of humor, but more importantly, a rather paranoid inability to understand subtlety. At the beginning of the play, when Linda tries to find a date for Allan, she asks what kind of girl he likes. His answer and disposition throughout most of the play is: "Little blondes with long hair and short skirts with big chests and boots, and a good behind. Something I can sink my teeth into." In his fantasies Allan has "tremendous poise," is an "absolute master." The women he dreams of are voluptuous and regarded by him as submissive sex objects. Finally the reason why he fails with Linda's friends is not so much that he is stumbling around, unable to live up to his masculine ideals, as that he is set on conquering them and thus incapable of treating them as human beings. When he does succeed with Linda, it is exactly because he does not see her as a thing to be subjugated.

The stoic Hollywood hero—it would seem—is neither a realistic nor ultimately a desirable model to emulate. In fact, Bogart calls to mind Mephistopheles when he sneaks in on Allan to offer his dubious advice. When Allan is finally not dragged off to Hell, but allowed merely to come down to reality, it is not because Woody Allen is a male chauvinist, but because Allan did not sell his soul and did not love and abandon scores of women—he only fantasized that he did. Of the Counter-Reformation myths, the one he resembles is finally not Faust and not Don Juan but clearly Don Quixote.

In the end, Allen deflates the very values these critics accuse him of holding. Indeed the ending of the movie version of *Play It Again, Sam!* (Allan Felix alone at the airport, capable at last of being himself for himself) calls to mind several of the women's pictures of the last couple of decades. One thinks of Claudia Weill's *Girlfriends* or Paul Mazursky's *An Unmarried Woman.* Finally, Allan Felix's ambivalence and insecurity about whether or not to live up to the standards of sexuality that are expected of him ought to evoke an even keener recognition from a female than from a male audience, since women have been struggling much more consciously with this dilemma, with "Cinderella Complexes" and "Superwoman Syndromes." What Woody Allen does is merely to present the problem of sexism as seen from the opposite point of view; what one might call the "Casanova Complex" or the "Superman Syndrome." Men seem to be as trapped in their role and no more comfortable with it than women are. Gornick's accusation is unjust because Allan Felix's "pursuit of women" is *supposed* to be "ridiculing."[2] But ultimately Allan himself is the one who is being ridiculed. Why else would he be "converted" in the end? Possibly the inability to distinguish between Allen and his fictional creation is what induces critics to accuse him of sexism instead of accusing his character.

In his essay "Comedy," Henri Bergson illustrates how the Don Quixote figure differs from a simpler comic hero: "Doubtless a fall is always a fall, but it is one thing to tumble into a well because you were looking anywhere but in front of you, it is quite another thing to fall into it because you were intent upon a star."[3] Where Axel Magee would fall into a well because he was clumsy, Allan

Felix—although he, too, is a *klutz*—does so because he does not pay attention to reality and so, in a sense, stumbles over it. The comedy of *Play It Again, Sam!* is based on the obvious disparity between Allan's Quixotic dreams of Hollywood machismo, and the reality of the sophisticated and independent women with whom he associates.

The majority of critics did identify with the Allen persona and his problems of discriminating between his dubious idealism and a not-so-gloomy reality. Richard Schickel epitomized the attitude of this group with his famous "Woody, c'est moi!" Another difference between the two types of comic figures that Bergson discusses is precisely the degree of identification they inspire in their audience. Oliver Hardy, who clearly belongs in the first category, once said of the two comic figures that he and Stan Laurel created: "Those two fellows . . . they are nice, very nice people. They never get anywhere because they are so dumb, but they don't know they're dumb. One reason why people like us, I guess, is because they feel superior to us."[4] Thus when we laugh at the clown who falls into the well because he is clumsy, we are at same time distanced from him in our superiority. When time and again the piano rolls down the stairs for Laurel and Hardy, we had already predicted it would happen and feel sure that it would never happen to us. Our laughter—to use Wisse's terms—contains more "merriment" than "harshness."

With the dreamer, on the other hand, we have a much greater sense of empathy because we identify with the very dreams that make him fall into the well in the first place. Thus his failure is painful to us, in a way that the slapstick clown's is not. Our laughter contains "harshness." Many of the greatest comics in movie history belong in this second category as does the classic *shlemiel* figure.[5] Audiences sympathize with the harassed dreamer. They recognize Chaplin's world, which is dictated by Adenoid Hynkel, and W. C. Fields' world, which is dominated by a nagging family. Allan Felix's real predicament is that he is doubly harassed: not only does he *live* in a mechanized and bureaucratized world, the *dreams* by means of which he tries to escape it are controlled by Hugh Hefner and Humphrey Bogart.

In Woody Allen's personal life three significant events occurred in the period around the opening of *Play It Again, Sam!:* his ex-wife Harlene Rosen sued him for defamation of character in the Heywood Allen routines; he met and employed Diane Keaton for the role of Linda Christie; and he and Louise Lasser separated. Their break-up, however, was not, according to Allen, hostile and definite the way that Allan and Nancy Felix's is, and there is not much reason to assume that the play is based on Allen's own experience except in the loosest way.

The year 1969 also saw the release of *Take the Money and Run,* the first movie over which Allen had complete artistic control. He wrote the screenplay (together with his friend Mickey Rose), directed it, and played the central character. *Take the Money and Run* is a spoof of two film genres: the documentary and the gangster film. In the form of the documentary, it presents Virgil Starkwell and his fictional life of crime. It thus juxtaposes the two sides of the classic cinematic dichotomy since the time of Lumière and Méliès—whether film should imitate reality or transform it—and plays them off against one another. One could even argue that the conjunction of the romanticism of the gangster genre versus the asserted neutral realism of the *cinema verité* reflects the Allen persona and his difficulty distinguishing between dream and reality.

Virgil Starkwell, like Allan Felix, is heavily influenced by Hollywood movies and cannot quite live up to the standards to which he aspires. He wants to become a "pool hustler and desperado," but from the very beginning of his career, he is a failure. Like the Allen *shlemiel*'s, his comedy is "existential" and derives, as Wisse said, from his confrontation with reality. As a child Virgil gets his hand caught in a gum-ball machine he is trying to rob. Later in life, he makes several abortive attempts at robbing banks, but fails in one case because he misspells the note he hands the teller, and in another because another gang has decided to rob the same bank, and the bank personnel would rather be robbed by the other gang. Despite the fact that he is thrown back into jail every time he manages to break out, Virgil is not discouraged in the least. At one point he tries to escape, but the pistol that he has carefully whittled out of a cake of soap and covered with shoe polish melts in the rain, and the guards take him back inside.

Virgil Starkwell is different from the Allen persona we have seen so far. He is a dreamer and a bungler, but he never deflates anybody, either by moral simplicity or by being snotty. His main similarity with the traditional *shlemiel* is that he never loses his faith; he may be timid, but he remains undaunted by the many defeats he suffers.

Although there are a few instances of slapstick in the film, the best of its humor is either verbal or caused by an imaginative disparity between the image and the asynchronous soundtrack. Jackson Beck—who did the original *Paramount Newsreels*—functions as the voice-over narrator. In addition to interviewing several people who used to know Virgil, Beck dogmatically comments on the filmclips we are shown. Yet, in a number of instances, his confident assertions are untrustworthy. In this manner the dictatorial "realism" of the documentary genre is rendered unreliable, and its conceit in assuming that it is omniscient is completely undermined. Although Virgil himself is not impertinent, the tables are ultimately turned on pomposity anyhow.

In one case we are told that Virgil's grandfather, of whom he was very fond, had an accident. He was hit in the head by a baseball, and, when he woke up, thought he was Kaiser Wilhelm and was committed to an insane asylum. What is shown is a faded film of the actual Kaiser and his army, while Beck claims that: "Here are some rare photos of him with patients on the sanatorium grounds." In another instance we are told that as a young boy Virgil received a cello as a gift while on the screen we see him stealing it in a store. The power of the voice-over is so strong that several critics have missed the information the image gives us and assumed that Virgil did in fact get his instrument as a gift. The joke is thus not only on the documentary genre, but also on the members of the audience who take it seriously.

This use of a comically contrapuntal soundtrack was further developed by editor Ralph Rosenblum. By January 1969, when production manager Jack Grossberg asked Rosenblum for help, the movie had been in the cutting room for eight months, and Palomar Pictures was considering not releasing it at all. Although the version he first saw was extremely uneven, Rosenblum agreed to re-edit it and Woody Allen's first movie was released after all. Apart from merely choosing, arranging, and rearranging shots, Rosenblum also worked on the soundtrack. The slow and solemn original music was replaced by cheerful Marvin Hamlisch tunes, and pieces of parallel soundtrack were removed and contrapuntal ones put in their place. In the scene where Virgil meets his future wife, Louise, for the first time, the romantic score that accompanied their walk through the park in a hazy light was replaced by a monologue in which Virgil tells us that "after fifteen minutes I wanted to marry her, and after a half hour I had completely given up the idea of snatching her purse."

One other vital element that Rosenblum changed in *Take the Money and Run!* was the ending. Allen had originally planned and filmed a last scene in which Virgil, after a bank robbery, is honeycombed by police bullets in the style of *Bonnie and Clyde*. This ending is illogical, not simply because the film is a comedy, but also because—as we shall see presently—it would have destroyed its integrity.

As is the nature of spoofs, *Take the Money and Run!* contains references, direct and indirect, to a number of films in the gangster genre. The scenes from the road gang parody similar scenes in the 1932 Paul Muni movie *I Am a Fugitive from a Chain Gang;* those where Virgil flees from state to state with his family, chased by the police, echo Fritz Lang's *You Only Live Once* from 1937. Also more contemporary films are comically imitated, most notably Arthur Penn's *Bonnie and Clyde* and Stuart Rosenberg's *Cool Hand Luke*—both of which were released in 1967 when Allen started working on the script for *Take the Money and Run*. Like Clyde Barrow, Virgil tries to boost his dubious manhood through the use of weapons. Unlike Clyde, he fails miserably: the switch blade flies out of his knife (an objective correllative of premature ejaculation, suggests Maurice Yacowar), and his gun turns out to be a cigarette lighter. Like Luke's, his punishment on the chain gang consists of several hours in the sweat box, only Allen has him locked up with an insurance salesman.

The two 1930s films that Allen parodies deviate from the standard 1930s gangster movie in that both of their heroes are innocent of the crimes they are convicted of. Both films are meant to illustrate the injustice of a society which is so obsessed with capturing un-American criminals that it will not give a formerly imprisoned man a chance to start over despite his honorable intentions and innocence. The prototypical gangster in films like *Little Caesar, Public Enemy,* and *Scarface,* despite the fact that he *is* guilty, never goes to jail. He is immune to the conventional legal system. As one scholar noted:

> What alarmed many concerned individuals at this time was that in this kind of film the police might just as well not have existed. Even though the gangsters usually killed only one another, they did so with a flagrant defiance of the law and with immunity from its penalties. As a result the contemporary American cities, whether Chicago, New York or unspecified, seemed wider open than the wildest frontier town of the Old West.[6]

In order to neutralize this immunity and satisfy the "concerned individuals" (read The Motion Picture Production Code), the final extermination of the gangster became necessary. If it was impossible to get him behind bars, the criminal would have to be annihilated. The reason why the early gangster is destroyed, then, is that he is successful. His liquidation is not simply practical—in that it gets him out of the way—but moral as well. As Robert Warshow suggested in his famous essay from 1948:

> At the bottom the gangster is doomed because he is under the obligation to succeed, not because the means he employs are unlawful. In the deeper layers of the modern consciousness, *all* means are unlawful, every attempt to succeed is an act of aggression, leaving one alone and guilty and defenseless among enemies: one is punished for success.[7]

When Bonnie and Clyde are also eliminated at the end of the 1960s movie, it is not so much a question of their being "punished for success." The values of the "modern consciousness" have obviously changed since Warshow's time, and reflecting the masochism that permeated much of the 1960s counterculture, Bonnie and Clyde's undoing *is* in fact their final achievement of success.

Whereas the goal of the mythical 1930s gangster was to gather excessive material wealth for himself and inspire awe in his peers, the archetypal 1960s outlaw is less financially ambitious and more vain. The ultimate sign of success for him is not fortune but fame, achieving celebrity, *becoming* mythical. Thus while we never see Bonnie and Clyde squandering after a robbery, we continually see them rummaging through newspapers to find their names and pictures. Toward the end of the film, Bonnie herself writes a poem about their adventures and sends it to the papers; when the poem is published and he is finally famous, Clyde overcomes his long impotence and shortly afterward the two of them are killed. Just like each one of the 1930s gangsters had his tragic flaw that led to his ultimate undoing, so Bonnie and Clyde's flaw appropriately is their narcissistic vanity.

For the 1930s audience the final destruction of the criminal supposedly signified the triumph of law and order: society was relieved of disruptive forces, and justice was being done. Although Bonnie and Clyde are outlaws as well, that status in the context of the 1960s is seen as infinitely preferable to the social order they are fleeing from. In fact, like a large segment of the movie audience at the time, they might more appropriately be termed dropouts. When they are killed, then, their destruction is seen not as justice, but as victimization.

The ending that Rosenblum decided to remove from *Take the Money and Run!* is ultimately illogical both in terms of the 1930s and the 1960s codes. Whereas Virgil Starkwell is as human as and a good deal more fallible than Bonnie and Clyde, the film he is in is not—as the ending would have suggested—a social critique. His status as outlaw is *not* fashionably self-imposed, but practical. It is his way of making a living. Unlike Tony Camonte, Little Caesar, Bonnie Parker and Clyde Barrow, Butch Cassidy and the Sundance Kid, Virgil Starkwell is unbelievably easy to get behind bars and his annihilation is thus redundant. It is equally unnecessary to punish him morally for his success. He does not have any. He was never a celebrity, although his wife would have liked him to be. As she tells the interviewer, "You know, he never made the Ten Most Wanted List. It's unfair voting. It's who you know."

The ending of the final product is completely in accordance with the film as a whole and very neatly ties up a number of its central themes. Throughout the movie Virgil Starkwell has been portrayed as the ultimate victim and outsider. His parents have disowned him and insist on wearing Groucho Marx noses and mustaches during their interviews. Everybody from the other members of his gang to the judge at his trial—and finally even himself while trying to appease an upset policeman—takes off his glasses and steps on them. And even though Virgil, as opposed to Heywood Allen, is actually a member of the "vegetable mentality" group, he is constantly cheated or humiliated by his fellow inmates. When he is finally captured and sentenced to 800 years in jail, the policeman who arrests him is one of his own friends.

In the final shot, Virgil is being interviewed in his cell. In the true spirit of the *shlemiel* character, he has not given up hope, but is whittling yet another bar of soap into the shape of a gun. When the interviewer asks him if he has regretted his life of crime, his reply reveals that—like Clyde Barrow—he is not sorry about his choice of career, and—unlike Clyde—he does not see his gangsterhood as a glamorous alternative lifestyle, but merely as a job:

> I think that crime definitely pays. And that, you know, it's a great job. The hours are good. And you're your own boss. And you travel a lot. And you get to meet interesting people. And I just think it's a good job in general. [Looking at his almost finished soap gun.] Do you know if it's raining out?

In 1971, the short pieces that Woody Allen had been writing for *The New Yorker* since the mid-1960s were published in a collection called *Getting Even*. In *Play It Again, Sam!* the dubious dreams of masculine superiority were deflated, and in *Take the Money and Run!* so was the pomposity of the documentary genre. In *Getting*

Even, the Allen persona makes fun of a large number of people, institutions, and phenomena that appeal to his pervasive sense of inferiority: the writing styles of famous novelists, quasi-intellectual overinterpretations of Hassidic tales and laundry lists, and witnesses at Nuremberg who "thought" that Hitler "worked for the phone company."[8] What is characteristic of the early essays, as of the early films, is the Allen persona's obsession with getting back at his physical, social, and intellectual superiors, with "getting even."

The essays are written partly in the tradition of Allen's predecessors Robert Benchley and S. J. Perelman, whose pieces appeared in *The New Yorker* in the 1930s, 1940s, and 1950s, and are partly inspired by Allen's own stand-up routines. Accordingly the characters in *Getting Even* can be divided into two distinct categories. One group consists of first person narrators who, although their circumstances seem similar to those of the Allen persona, sound more like the narrative voice in Perelman's stories than like Heywood Allen or Virgil Starkwell. The other group of characters superficially seem very different from Allen's *shlemiel,* but turn out, through the simplicity of their language, to resemble him much more.

Although Heywood Allen also worked in the first person, his routines were meant to be heard. The language in the first person written pieces is considerably more complex precisely because it is meant to be read. It is strictly literary and highly stylized. In the stand-up routines, when Heywood is attacked by a "Neanderthal man" in his lobby at two o'clock in the morning, he describes it thus:

> I took out my watch, and I dangled it in front of him, you know. They're mollified by shiny objects sometimes. . . . He ate it.

Compare the linguistic simplicity of this routine with the complexity in an essay like "Viva Vargas!" when the rebels are ambushed:

> This was partially my fault as I gave away our position by inadvertently shrieking out the names of the Christian triumvirate when a tarantula crawled over my leg. For several moments I could not dislodge the tenacious little spider as it made its way into the inner recesses of my garments, causing me to gyrate spastically toward the stream and thrash in it for what seemed like forty-five minutes.[9]

When both excerpts are set side by side with a typical piece of

Perelmanesque, there can be no doubt who the "Viva Vargas" persona derives from:

> We had crawled back to Bombay from New Delhi in a state of bleary disrepair, thoroughly dehydrated by the savage midsummer heat but starry-eyed at the prospect of quitting India, when kismet, working hand in glove with the steamship company, had again put her knee into our groin.[10]

The other group of characters who do sound like the Allen *shlemiel* do so for linguistic rather than adventitious reasons. Among them are such unlikely figures as Count Dracula, Rabbis Ben Kaddish, Raidtz of Poland, and Baumel, and Death. They are not narrators but part of a plot, and thus they speak in everyday dialogue.

In the one act play "Death Knocks" (all of which is, of course, dialogue), Death—in spite of somberly resembling the death figure in Ingmar Bergman's *The Seventh Seal*, turns out to be, like Nat Ackerman whom he has come to pick up, a middle-aged, irritating *kvetch* who speaks with a Brooklyn inflection. Although he does not like the idea of dying, Nat is not particularly afraid of this death figure. He suggests—like Bergman's knight—that they play chess so that he can gain another twenty-four hours. This Death does not play chess, though, so they decide on gin rummy, a game that is much more in accordance with his intelligence. Nat wins not only an extra day but twenty-eight dollars. Death is devastated: "I'm stranded. . . . Where's a good hotel? What am I talking about hotel, I got no money. I'll go sit in Bickford's."[11]

Like Heywood Allen in the "Deep South" routine, Nat Ackerman outwits Death by his simplicity. Although he is afraid of dying, Nat nevertheless deflates and humiliates Death. Death says, "I remind him of [his good friend] Moe Lefkowitz. I'm one of the most terrifying figures you could possibly imagine, and I remind him of Moe Lefkowitz."[12]

All through *Getting Even,* the subjects of death and dying are ridiculed and referred to jokingly. In "My Philosophy" one of the Aphorisms goes: "It is impossible to experience one's own death objectively and still carry a tune."[13] In "Conversations with Helmholtz" we are told that "Freud's death, according to Ernest Jones, was the event that caused the final break between Helmholtz and Freud and the two rarely spoke afterwards."[14]

Unlike the stand-up routines, the deflating in *Getting Even* goes beyond the Allen persona's personal "enemies." Thus, in addition to Death and the "pioneers of psychoanalysis," such celebrities as J. P. Morgan, Robert E. Lee, Hess, Göring, and Hitler are ridiculed. Yet again, as in *Take the Money and Run!*, there is no indication that *Getting Even* is meant as social criticism. As Allen himself said in an interview:

> I'm a firm believer that art is not a useful thing regarding social change. It's pure entertainment, and that goes for opera, drama, classical music, painting. . . . If your entertainment sensibilities are on a high level, you listen to more complex and sophisticated artists. Comedy least of all. People always think the way to attack a social problem is to laugh at it and satirize it. I say that's pure entertainment. You show how pompous and ridiculous the Nazis are and they still come and kill you.[15]

The essays are intended purely as comedy and meant—as the title suggests—to mock and retaliate rather than to subvert and eradicate. The title of this collection neatly sums up the major concern of the early, insecure Allen persona: getting even, achieving personal revenge and satisfaction.

In 1971 Woody Allen's second film, *Bananas* also was released. Because of its thematic similarities with two subsequent films, *Sleeper* (1973) and *Love and Death* (1975), discussion of it will be deferred for a while.

Meanwhile Allen's third movie, *Everything You Always Wanted to Know About Sex*, came out in 1972—the same year that the film version of *Play It Again, Sam!* was released. The film is based on the title of David Reuben's bestseller rather than the actual book, and consists of seven short sketches that attempt to answer questions about various aspects of sexual normality and abnormality such as: "What Is Sodomy?" "Are Transvestites Homosexuals?" and "What Happens During Ejaculation?"

Like *Play It Again, Sam!* and *Take the Money and Run!*, this movie is deeply rooted in the realm of Hollywood, and each sketch is a spoof of a film genre. The first is an imitation of a medieval romance, and the last takes place in a futuristic looking brain "control room" of a man who is about to have sex. In between the remote Elizabethan past and the science fiction future, other genres such as the Hollywood romance, the horror movie, and the Italian art film are mocked.

Like *Don't Drink the Water!*, *Everything You Always Wanted to Know About Sex* is not centered around the Allen persona. We do, however, see glimpses of him, and Allen plays a number of roles in the various sketches. He opens the film playing the medieval counterpart to the stand-up comedian: the court jester. The jester has based his entire repertory on jokes that deflate the king, and all through the sketch the jester is trying, by means of an aphrodisiac (the topic of the sketch), to seduce the queen. While the potion does work, the intrigue is exposed by the king, and the jester is decapitated in a scene which is clearly a homage to Orson Welles's *Othello*.

In the third sketch, Allen plays an Italian whose wife can only have sex in public places—he even speaks Italian in it. In the sixth he is trying to catch a man-size female breast which has escaped from the research laboratory of a mad sexual scientist. Finally, in the last sketch he plays "sperm no. 2" who is extremely worried that now he has to act on the oath he took in training school that he would "fertilize an ovum or die trying."

There is no doubt that *Everything You Always Wanted to Know About Sex* is one of Woody Allen's weakest movies. The king's evaluation of the jester's jokes in the first sketch—"Not funny!"—is indeed quite a good introduction to the film as a whole. It is visually more interesting than the other films up until that point, but Allen seems to have put so much effort into improving the cinematic aesthetics that the comedy is neglected. Its script, as some critics have suggested, may indeed be funnier to read than the film is to watch: whereas the idea of a man having intercourse with a large rye bread, a rabbi who is turned on by being whipped while his wife is sitting at his feet eating pork, or a colossal breast ravaging a whole county may be amusing, actually watching these ideas is not comical in the least, but seems rather adolescent.

The one sketch that makes the film worth watching is the one called "What Is Sodomy?"—a story, told with a surprising amount of pathos, of a well-to-do doctor who falls in love with a sheep. All the standard clichés of romantic melodrama are used here in a completely warped fashion, as when Gene Wilder (in the best performance of his entire career) says to Daisy, the sheep, "I know it must all seem strange to you. Me from Jackson Heights and you from the hills of Armenia. And yet, I think it could work if we gave it a chance."

In terms of David Reuben's book, the film demonstrates, as Diane Jacobs has suggested, "that it's absurd, not to mention unerotic, to presume that one can be *told* everything one wants to know about sex."[16] In terms of Allen's works, the most interesting thing about *Everything You Always Wanted to Know About Sex* is its irreverent, unrestrained treatment of the taboo subject of sex. Death, as we saw, is minimized and deflated in Allen's early work whereas sex is blown out of all proportion, as visualized by the enormous breast and the erection, in the last sketch, which requires a crane. The two subjects of death and sex and the relationship between them have played an important part in most of Allen's subsequent work.

3
Among the Very Young at Heart?
(1971–1976)

Ah, the bravery you tell yourself was possible when it's all over,
the bravery of the staircase.[1]
                                          —Lillian Hellman

Despite the fact that *Bananas* is set in contemporary Latin America, *Sleeper* in totalitarian America in the twenty-second century, and *Love and Death* in czarist Russia, these films have a number of factors in common. In all three, the Allen persona is placed in an environment which is unfamiliar to him and with which he is forced to cope. We experience his alienation in the past, the present, and the future. Also in all three films the private sphere is shown as infinitely preferable to the public, and personal relationships as superior to politics. Finally, all three films are deeply rooted in the American cinematic comic tradition in a way which Allen's other films are not.

As Jackson Beck constituted a narrative frame for *Take the Money and Run,* so Roger Grimsby and Howard Cosell do for *Bananas.* In the opening scene of Woody Allen's second movie, ABC's *Wide World of Sports* transmits a "live on-the-spot assassination" of the president of San Marcos, a Latin American banana republic.[2] Howard Cosell bends over the dying man and says, "When did you know it was all over?"

When his relationship with politically active Nancy ends, Fielding Mellish decides to go on their planned vacation to San Marcos alone. After many complications, he ends up in the camp of Esposito and his rebels, who are planning to overthrow the dictator who was behind the coup in the first scene. The guerillas are democratic humanists, but after a messy and all but accidental revolution on Esposito's orders they start relentlessly executing the former government. They realize that Esposito's power has

47

gone to his head and urge Fielding to become the new president of San Marcos. He reluctantly agrees, only to find out that his first assignment is an official visit to the United States. Despite his fake Fidel Castro beard, Fielding is exposed as an imposter and given a suspended sentence provided that he promise never to move into the judge's neighborhood. His trial, like his subsequent wedding night with Nancy, is covered by Howard Cosell and ABC's *Wide World of Sports*.

The plot of *Sleeper* is similar, but where Fielding's precarious situation to a certain extent was self-imposed, Miles Monroe's is utterly involuntary. He wakes up in the year 2173 and realizes that his doctors had frozen him by mistake when he went in for a check-up two hundred years earlier. The new government has "electronically simplified" the entire population of America, and *Sleeper* begins where *Invasion of the Body Snatchers* left off. Miles agrees, again reluctantly, to cooperate with subversive elements. Disguised as a domestic robot, he hides in the household of vacant poet Luna Schlosser, who, after serious misgivings, decides to help him against the police. After a long chase sequence, Miles is caught and Luna joins the guerilas. The government simplifies Miles's brain, and he quickly adjusts to his new situation. To make sure he is completely "simplified," the scientists put him in a Miss America contest which he wins. Luna and Erno, the rebel leader, kidnap Miles and manage to shatter his simplified personality by reenacting some of the major traumas of his life.

Erno informs Miles that there has been a successful attempt on The Leader's life and that all that is left of the fascist dictator is his nose, from which a team of doctors are trying to restore the man using cloning. Disguised as doctors, Miles and Luna, on Erno's orders, force their way into the hospital and steal the nose, which they throw in front of a steam roller.

In the last scene, Miles tries to persuade Luna to fall in love with him instead of "tall blonde, Prussian, Nordic, Aryan Nazi type" Erno. "In six months," he tells her, "we'll be stealing Erno's nose. Political solutions don't work! It doesn't matter who's up there, they're all terrible." Luna answers, "You don't believe in science, you don't believe in political systems, and you don't believe in God, huh? So then, what do you believe in?" Miles's reply ends the movie: "Sex and Death. Two things that come once in my lifetime. But at least after death you're not nauseous."

In *The Culture of Narcissism*, Christopher Lasch argues that in a "warlike society" the dominant personality type is "at heart antisocial" and tends to see others in the same way, "as basically dishonest and unreliable." The result of this attitude, according to Lasch, is a "cult of personal relations, which becomes increasingly intense as the hope of political solutions recedes."[3]

Miles's narcissistic conclusion also applies to the Allen persona in *Bananas* and—as we shall see—*Love and Death*. Although a noble and democratic man before the revolution, Esposito turned out to be worse than Vargas as soon as he tasted the sweets of power.[4] Likewise Boris in *Love and Death* is certain that fighting for the czar against Napoleon is absurd: "They're both crooks. The czar is a little taller."[5] In all three films, the Allen persona's belief in personal relationships—love or sex as the matter may be—is visualized and grossly overstated. The shot where Fielding is taking off his clothes to make love to Yolanda, a female rebel, is filmed in slow motion and accompanied by Tchaikovsky's *1812 Overture;* the copulation thus takes on the dimension of Napoleon entering Moscow. Similarly his wedding night with Nancy is transmitted on national television.

The narcissist is by definition the complete antithesis to the *shlemiel* character, and although the Allen figure has several narcissistic traits in these early films, he is still basically a *shlemiel*. Thus his belief in personal relationships is seen not so much as a reflection of the persona's inner emptiness and isolation, but rather as a lovable characteristic in a person who is capable of retaining his capacity for love, hope, and faith in a crazy world, as illustrated in the Marvin Hamlisch song that is played over the end credits in *Bananas*, " 'Cause I believe in loving, some people take me for a fool. . . ." Likewise Miles's anschauung in *Sleeper:* despite the fact that he has not had sex in 200 years, ("204 if you count my marriage") and that science has proven, so Luna tells him, that "meaningful relationships between men and women don't last," Miles still believes in love and sex. Like the *shlemiel,* he refuses to give up his faith just because science has proved otherwise.

In spite of their many thematic similarities, *Bananas* and *Sleeper* are quite different in terms of style and comic origins. In *Bananas* we find a number of direct, although rather esoteric, references to works of other filmmakers; serious (Bergman and Eisenstein) as well as comic. When Fielding is demonstrating the "Execucizer" (an exercise machine for executives) at the beginning of the film, he brings to mind Chaplin's Tramp with the feeding device in *Modern Times*. Likewise, when Fielding is nearly trampled to death by fellow demonstrators outside the embassy he is picketing, he is as out of place as the Tramp when he accidentally picks up the red banner. Similarly the opening scene of *The Great Dictator* is invoked when Fielding is training with the guerillas.

These slapstick incidents, however, are exceptions rather than rules. The comic tradition which *Bananas* belongs to is not the silent tradition of Chaplin, but the highly verbal one of Bob Hope, W. C. Fields, and especially Groucho Marx. Thus the frantically exaggerated impression of the political situation in Latin America in *Bananas* calls to mind the zaniness of the war in Fredonia in *Duck Soup.* The most vivid example of this is Fielding's trial toward the end of the film. Fielding calls it a "travesty of a mockery of a sham," and hysterically runs in and out of the witness stand to question himself. One witness mysteriously teaches evolution, and a black woman presents herself as (and actually resembles) J. Edgar Hoover. The members of the jury are smoking pot, and one of them is drinking out of a fish bowl with a straw.

Sleeper is fundamentally different from *Bananas* and rather atypical in terms of Allen's work in that its humor is almost entirely visual. It is, as Allen said, "a picture that every kid from five or six to thirteen could see and find funny."[6] The incidents of verbal comedy are rare, unmotivated, and far outweighed by the slapstick scenes. It is also worth noting that whereas in *Bananas* Allen used the extremely verbal Louise Lasser, in *Sleeper* the leading lady is played by the all but inarticulate Diane Keaton. Miles Monroe is less of a con man than his predecessors and has much more in common with the silent clowns, Keaton and the early Chaplin. Of the Marx Brothers the one that he calls to mind—for instance in the opening scene—is Harpo.

Apart from the many chase scenes in which the bungling policemen echo the Keystone Cops, the greatest slapstick cliché of all times is grossly caricatured in a scene where Miles goes out to procure food for himself and Luna and sees a field of vegetables and fruits as big as himself. He starts peeling a banana, but is discovered by an angry peasant who runs after him. Fielding throws his banana and both of them start slipping on the six foot banana peel. The scene is completely predictable and yet so gross that it is utterly surprising.

The basic thematic concerns of both *Bananas* and *Sleeper* resemble those of Chaplin's films. Allen's *shlemiel,* like Chaplin's Tramp, is placed in an environment which is less sensitive than he is and therefore hostile toward him—a common enough theme in Jewish culture. Like Heywood Allen, Fielding and Miles are confronted with what Chaplin called the "accumulating complexities of modern life, . . . gigantic institutions that threaten from all sides."[7]

Chaplin's little barber ends *The Great Dictator* with his speech to Hannah: a fervent, sentimental, and slightly platitudinous speech that is full of hope for a decent future for the human race despite the threat of Nazism. The Allen persona is not nearly as noble as Chaplin's Tramp. Although he too wants a world in which it is possible to retain human dignity and believe and say what you want without being persecuted for it, he wants it primarily for himself. His concerns are much more narcissistically directed. (Again we see a conflict between the *shlemiel* and the narcissist in the early Allen persona.) Thus, when Fielding has a chance to "die for freedom," his reaction is, "That's swell. Freedom is wonderful. On the other hand if you're dead . . . it's a tremendous drawback to your sex life." And Miles's speech to Luna at the end of *Sleeper* is considerably less sublime than the barber's. What he believes in has to do not with the human race, but with his private self.

In an interview in connection with *Sleeper,* Woody Allen said, "The contemporary conflicts are within yourself. They're neurotic conflicts between you and your girlfriend, or you and your parents. They're not conflicts of the Depression, or having to make a living, or guys working in factories. They're much less clearly visual, much more subtle . . . and very hard for a comedian to get a grip on without simply doing verbal comedy, . . . so we get reduced to seeking content sources in secondary material."[8]

Even in the early films that are based on "secondary material," it is evident that what Allen is working toward is a visualization of the "contemporary conflicts," which are also, by the way, the conflicts of the narcissist. Consequently the most convincing scenes in the early works have to do with the Allen persona's conflict with his parents and his woman friend. Although these scenes are often peripheral to the plot, they are in accordance with the narcissism of the Allen persona and his preference for the private as opposed to the public world, personal relationships as opposed to political solutions.

In *Take the Money and Run,* Virgil, during his first date with Louise, wants to pay her a compliment. He tells her that he likes the new hat she is wearing, "That's a pretty hat. I see them all over town. . . . They're on sale. . . . There are millions of them. You know in one of those bins." Though Louise, being relatively normal, looks slightly annoyed by his remark, Virgil's intentions are good. To him, the eternal outsider, the notion of conformity is comforting and his comment is affectionately meant. In a similar scene in *Bananas,* Nancy wants to break up their relationship but because she is embarrassed she makes Fielding try to guess why. "No," she replies in answer to his frantic surmises, "it has nothing to do with the fact that your teeth are in bad shape." Although Allen's concern with "contemporary conflicts" constitutes but a minor part of the early films, it is their most highly original element as well as the genesis to Allen's later, more idiosyncratic and mature work.

Also in terms of cinematic form there is a clear development at this point in Allen's career. Where *Take the Money and Run!* and *Bananas,* despite their very controlled editing, look as dishevelled and slapped together as a Marx Brothers movie, *Sleeper* is much more disciplined and visually fastidious than the other two films. Allen started paying attention to picture compositon and hired photographer David M. Walsh, whom he also used on *Everything You Always Wanted to Know About Sex.* Nevertheless, Allen's first two movies are much more stimulating and funny than either *Sex* or *Sleeper.* Not so much because, as Allen has often surmised, highly developed cinematic style is antithetical to comedy, but rather because slapstick happens not to be his natural domain. Woody Allen's talent is his verbal, definitely not his physical, agility.

In his fifth film, *Love and Death,* Allen more successfully combines his newly acquired cinematic skills with his own comic form, the verbal comedy. The result is his funniest movie to date. From its title we already sense that it is going to be different from and slightly more introspective than the earlier films. This surmise is supported by the opening words of Boris, the central character of the movie:

> How I got into this predicament I'll never know. Absolutely incredible. To be executed for a crime I never committed. Of course isn't all mankind in the same boat? Isn't all mankind ultimately executed for a crime it never committed? The difference is that all man go eventually, but I go six o'clock tomorrow morning.

But if Boris's narration supports our impression that this film is going to be more serious, the delightfully sprightly music from Prokofiev's *Lieutenant Kije* suite undermines it. The film in its entirely is characterized by a similar construction: each time a philosophical issue is introduced, it is immediately undermined by a joke.

Boris proceeds to narrate his autobiography. He was always the outsider in his family. While his two brothers were fighting and playing games, Boris had a "completely different concept of my-self." From the image of the two boys fighting, the film cuts to Boris as a child hanging on a cross. When Napoleon invades Russia, the three brothers, much to unmartial Boris's regret, have to go to war. Yet while his courageous brother Ivan gets killed, Boris unbelievably becomes a hero. During a battle he hides in a cannon, falls asleep, and is fired into the enemy headquarters. Also by pure accident he survives a duel and marries his lovely cousin Sonia, who has been sleeping with half of Moscow.

After much tension and unhappiness, their marriage becomes very idyllic. When Napoleon invades Russia again, Sonia suggests that together they assassinate the disturber of their peace. Because Boris cannot quite convince himself that killing is justifiable ac-cording to his messy philosophical standards, somebody else does it instead, only the man who is assassinated is not Napoleon but his double. The ultimate absurdity of Boris's situation, then, is that not only is he arrested and convicted for a murder he did not commit, the crime was, in fact, not committed at all. Napoleon is not dead.

While Boris is awaiting his execution, an angel of God tells him not to worry, he will be pardoned. Apparently the angel was misinformed, however, and Boris is shot as planned. When he goes to bid Sonia farewell, he tells her that he "got screwed" and that being dead is worse than "the chicken at Tresky's." Finally, he turns to the audience with his ultimate excogitation on love and death, and then, echoing the ending of Ingmar Bergman's *The Seventh Seal,* he waltzes off with the whiteclad death figure, accom-panied once more by Prokofiev's "Troika":

> The question is, have I learned anything about life? Only that human beings are divided into mind and body. The mind embraces all the nobler aspirations, like poetry and philosophy, but the body has all the fun. The important thing, I think, is not to be bitter. . . . After all, you know, there are worse things in life than death. I mean, if you've ever spent an evening with an insurance salesman, you know exactly what I mean. . . . Regarding love, you know, uh, what can you say? It's the, it's not the quantity of your sexual relations that count, it's the quality. On the other hand, if the quantity drops below once every eight months, I would definitely look into it. Well, that's about it for me, folks. Goodbye.

Love and Death has a number of mutual concerns with *Bananas* and *Sleeper.* Like Fielding and Miles, Boris is placed in a hostile environment. Although he is supposedly gentile, he is still a *shlemiel* and an outsider, and after all, what could be a more suitable nineteenth-century environment for a *shlemiel* than Russia? In effect Boris is a twentieth-century New York Jew who has been misplaced. Thus, he asks his cousin Sonia: "You dating any Russians that I should know about?" When relatives tell him that she is "taking lovers," he misunderstands because of their heavy Russian accent, and his astonished reply is "She's taking uppers?" When they take him to see Mozart's *The Magic Flute,* his reaction is: "It's a helluvan opera, isn't it? . . . Do they sell popcorn or gumdrops or something?"

Also like his predecessors, Boris does not believe in politics. The czar and Napoleon are not only "crooks," but completely ridiculous. Napoleon's greatest worry is whether he will be able to invent the "Napoleon" before the English invent "Beef Wellington." The war is equally ludicrous. Human lives are wasted to no purpose. The brave Ivan gets killed and the coward Boris becomes a hero. During the battles there are cheerleaders and people selling popcorn, and at one point the film cuts from a shot of soldiers fighting to one of baaing sheep.

Nevertheless, *Love and Death* is not an antiwar film as such, just as *Bananas* and *Sleeper* are not political films. In an interview in connection with the release of *Love and Death,* Woody Allen said, "I'm not subverting. I'm complaining."[9] This is a very precise delineation of Allen's early works. The comedy of the *shlemiel* is not a revolutionary comedy, but rather one that is used as a means of surviving by "getting even." The Allen persona is not obliterating but merely *kvetching.* Furthermore, in his innocence the *shlemiel* figure is totally incapable of understanding the mechanisms of war. There is an old Yiddish story about the battle of Tannenberg in which the *shlemiel* sounds remarkably like Boris. The officer tells his company: "The moment has come! We're going to charge the enemy. It'll be man against man in hand to hand combat." The *shlemiel* replies: "Please, sir, show me my man! Perhaps I can come to an understanding with him."[10] In a parallel scene in Allen's film, the officer tells his men that they are going to war. The side that kills the most men from the other side will win. Boris incomprehendingly asks: "What do we win?" The *shlemiel,* although he may be a coward in everybody else's eyes, is, in ours, the only sane man in a world where war, not peace, is the normal state.

Love and Death deviates from Allen's earlier works on a number of crucial points, however, all of which show a development away from his original *shlemiel* persona. In addition to his hostile surroundings, Boris has another "enemy," a cruel and inhumane universe. His is a protest not so much against Napoleon and the czar and their morally reprehensible politics, but rather against the unfairness of the fact that all mankind is "ultimately executed for a crime it never committed." Although (again like the narcissist) he is much more concerned with the fact that he goes "six o'clock tomorrow morning" than with the fact that "all men go eventually." Accordingly, Allen, paraphrasing Tolstoy, said to his biographer Eric Lax, "Any man over thirty-five with whom death is not the main consideration is a fool. The enemy is God and nature and the universe—that's what's killing us. The enemy is not the Chinese or the guy next door. The enemy is out there."[11]

Because of his knowledge that he is going to die, happiness is not possible for Boris. When his marriage with Sonia is harmonious and blissful, Boris suddenly gets depressed and feels an uncontrollable urge to kill himself. In Tolstoy's *Anna Karenina,* one of the works that *Love and Death* parodies, Levin, in a similar situation, has to "hide a rope lest he be tempted to hang himself."[12] Boris does hang himself, but, while dangling from his rope, suddenly starts thinking about oral sex and cuts himself down. (One might mention that Lasch names oral cravings as one of the chief characteristics of the narcissist.) When Sonia moans that the only truly happy person she knows is their friend the village idiot, Boris replies, "Well, it's easy to be happy, you know, if your one concern in life is figuring out how much saliva to dribble."

In answer to a question about Allen's personal psychological state, his friend and the co-writer of a number of his filmscripts, Marshall Brickman, said, "The happy/unhappy axis is a fallacy in contemporary society. The point is to be awake, alert, functioning."[13] The conclusion is that in the Allenesque universe, happiness is perhaps not such a desirable state after all. Just as intelligence leads to disillusion and skepticism, so happiness automatically entails imbecility.

Finally, *Love and Death* differs from Allen's previous work in that Boris does not manage to outwit death. Death, in effect, outwits him: although he is promised a pardon by God, he is executed. Or, as he tells Sonia, "I got screwed." Unlike Heywood Allen in the "Deep South" routine or Nat Ackerman in "Death Knocks," Boris is ultimately forced to go with the white clad figure. "The important thing," he tells us, "is not to be bitter."

Despite the introduction of gloomier subjects into *Love and Death,* however, it remains Allen's funniest movie to date. Mainly

this is because Woody Allen, as he admitted, "subordinates everything to the laugh" in it.[14] Thus the rather pessimistic notion that
"there's somebody—or something—out there who for some irrational unexplainable reason is killing us,"[15] is well hidden underneath an abundance of funny lines. Accordingly, when Boris and
Sonia start meditating about life and death, they always get side-
tracked and their ideas are turned into jokes. Thus Boris says, "I
am consumed with remorse, and stricken with suffering for the
human race. Not only that, but, I'm developing, ah, a herpes on,
on my lip here that is really killing me." This may be another
esoteric reference to Tolstoy's *Anna Karenina*. After Anna's suicide, Vronsky's mother tells a friend: "For six weeks he never said
a word to anyone, and would not touch food. . . . He went raving
mad, almost. . . . He is so miserable. And added to his other
miseries he has a toothache."[16]

Also in 1975 Woody Allen published his second collection of
essays, *Without Feathers*. Like *Getting Even*, *Without Feathers* makes
fun of topics like quasi-intellectual overinterpretations of Irish
poetry and nitpicking speculations over who actually wrote Shakespeare's plays. Like *Love and Death*, however, it deviates from the
fundamental *shlemiel* figure, and the best of the essays—and the
two plays that take up half of the volume—are constructed in a
comic fashion similar to that of the movie.

The title of the book is inspired by a poem by Emily Dickinson
that reads: "Hope is the thing with feathers." Being without feathers, then, means being without hope. Since hope is one of the
intrinsic ingredients in the comedy of the Yiddish *shlemiel,* this
collection is clearly a departure from Allen's previous works although the Allen persona is still a *shlemiel* in the sense of "bungler." Yet, no sooner is this general sense of hopelessness
expressed by the title than it is deflated. In the first essay, "Selec-
tions from the Allen Notebooks," the narrator says: "How wrong
Emily Dickinson was! Hope is not 'the thing with feathers.' The
thing with feathers has turned out to be my nephew. I must take
him to a specialist in Zurich."[17]

Another elementary quality which characterizes the *shlemiel* is
his faith. This characteristic has likewise been relinquished in
Without Feathers. Thus the "Proverb" that reads "The lion and the
calf shall lie down together but the calf won't get much sleep."[18]
Even one of the classic examples of faith is toyed with, namely
Abraham's willingness to sacrifice his son at the Lord's command:

> And so he took Isaac to a certain place and prepared to sacrifice him
> but at the last minute the Lord stayed Abraham's hand and said, "How
> could thou doest such a thing?"

And Abraham said, "But thou said—"

"Never mind what I said," the Lord spake. Doth thou listen to every crazy idea that comes thy way?"

And Abraham grew ashamed. "Er—not really—no."

"I jokingly suggest thou sacrifice Isaac and thou immediately runs out to do it."

And Abraham fell to his knees, "See, I never know when you're kidding."

And the Lord thundered, "No sense of humor. I can't believe it."[19]

Two other concerns of *Love and Death,* which reappear in these essays, are God and death. Both subjects are repeatedly presented in a serious manner, and then deflated by a joke. The persona asks, "And how can I believe in God when just last week I got my tongue caught in the roller of an electric typewriter. I am plagued by doubts. What if everything is an illusion and nothing exists? In that case, I definitely overpaid for my carpet."[20] And later he says, "The thing is to remember that each time of life has its proper rewards, whereas if you're dead it's hard to find the light switch. The chief problem about death, incidentally, is the fear that there may be no afterlife—a depressing thought, particularly for those who have bothered to shave. Also, there is the fear that there is an afterlife but no one will know where it's being held."[21]

In *Love and Death* and *Without Feathers,* as in the previous works, the Allen persona is trying hard to "get even." Yet in the earlier works, the deflating was done randomly and was aimed at a number of people, institutions, and aspects of modern life which made the Allen persona feel inferior. In the two later works, what he tried frantically to debunk is very specifically God, death, and the hopelessly empty universe. The "Getting Even" syndrome of the early works has here taken on a further dimension, the "Without Feathers" aspect. The Allen persona no longer deflates by haphazardly rapping out nasty remarks, but by bathetically juxtaposing hope, faith, God, and death with such trivialities as shaving and finding the light switch.

In the two one-act plays, the titles of which are precisely "God" and "Death," these themes are treated relatively more seriously. "God" is the more imaginative, but in terms of the Allen persona, the least interesting of the two. It is set in Athens in 500 B.C. and in the course of the play, or rather a play within the play, God is not only rendered untrustworthy as in *Love and Death* but actually dies, in a most undignified manner. He is strangled by the "deus ex machina" contraption. The anarchic absurdity, which in *Love and Death* was used to emphasize the sense of chaos in the universe, is here exaggerated even further so as to produce the feeling that its ruler is indeed not God, but more probably Harpo Marx.

In "Death" the protagonist, Kleinman, is awakened in the middle of the night by upset neighbors who tell him that a maniacal killer is on the loose and force him to go out with them to try and catch him. The vigilantes have a plan, but as one of them tells Kleinman:

> Each of us only knows one small fraction of the overall plan at any given moment—his own assignment. . . . It's a precaution against the maniac finding out the plan. . . . [It] can't be either carelessly disclosed or given up under duress or threat. Each one can only account for a tiny fragment which would have no meaning to the maniac should he gain access to it. Clever?[22]

The problem is that the plan is so clever that Kleinman is never able to find out exactly what his assignment is. Gradually, as the group gets more and more paranoid about the identity of the murderer, it starts breaking up, and factions form. Kleinman is accused of being the killer, and is just about to be executed by his friends when a messenger arrives to inform them that the maniac has been trapped somewhere else. After they have all gone off to find him, Kleinman is caught by the maniac, who turns out to be his spitting image, and is stabbed to death.

The killer, as we gradually understand, is death. Like Nat Ackerman in "Death Knocks," Kleinman finds that his death resembles him, but like Boris in *Love and Death*, he is incapable of escaping. Kleinman does indeed have more in common with Boris than with Nat. Whereas Nat Ackerman outwits Death with his *shlemiel* simplicity and innocence, Kleinman is frightened of death, and aware of the potential danger. He is, like Boris, a philosophizing coward. He keeps insisting that he does not want to get involved, either in catching the murderer or in the bigger questions about the mystery of the universe: "I'm a man who likes to know which way is up and which way is down and where's the bathroom."[23]

At this point in Allen's career, his persona has shed his *shlemiel* role, and with it his innocence, his faith, and his hope. In Woody Allen's next film, *Annie Hall*, the male character Alvy Singer is developed one step further from the *shlemiel*, and Allen himself partially stops subordinating "everything to the laugh." But before he went on to his own next project, Allen played the title role in Martin Ritt's movie *The Front*.

Despite all his frustrations over *What's New, Pussycat?* and *Casino*

Royale, Woody Allen decided to act in a film that he did not direct. This time it was a completely different undertaking from Feldman's million dollar movies. Martin Ritt's *The Front* deals with the moral implications of the 1950s McCarthyism witch hunts, and several of the actors, as well as the scriptwriter, Walter Bernstein, and Ritt himself were actually blacklisted at the time.

Although he was uncomfortable about not being in control of the project, Allen was persuaded by its topic. The McCarthy period, he says, "is a shameful era and one that has never been explored."[24] Also the thought of a film in which "I didn't constantly have to go for the gags was tempting."[25] Ultimately *The Front,* for precisely those reasons became a turning point in his career.

The Front opens with Frank Sinatra's 1953 hit *Young at Heart* played over a montage of old filmclips showing, among other things, the wedding of Joseph McCarthy, bombings of Korea, a ticker-tape parade for General MacArthur, the Eisenhowers entertaining guests, and Julius and Ethel Rosenberg being led into a paddy wagon.

Its plot begins when a television writer, Alfred Miller, gets blacklisted. In his desperation, he asks the most unpolitical, unintellectual friend he has to be his front. Alfred writes the scripts, and Howard Prince submits them to the television network. Howard, who works as a cashier at the "Friendly Tavern" and is a bookmaker on the side, willingly agrees to help his friend, partly because Alfred pays him 10 percent of his salary. Before long Howard is a front for three writers and famous all over the country. But while "Howard's" shows get top ratings, its leading actor, a burlesque *Borscht Belt* style comedian, Hecky Brown, gets blacklisted. He is told that he will be able to work only if he cooperates with the "Freedom Information Service" and he spies on Howard Prince to see if the new genius shows any un-American tendencies.

Howard, in the meantime, is falling in love with pretty and intelligent Florence Barrett, a script editor at the network, who is as sincerely outraged by the inquisitions as Howard is indifferent to them. She decides to give up her job because she will no longer be a silent bystander. When she proudly comes to Howard's apartment to tell him of her decision, his complete passivity makes her scream at him: "We live in the world, Howard!" Howard's reply reflects his pride in his new luxurious apartment, which Florence has not yet commented on, as well as his unwillingness to get involved: "*You* live in the world; I live right here."[26]

Howard turns out to be not nearly as safe as he thinks he is, however. Hecky manages to produce enough evidence against him so that the House Un-American Activities Committee can subpoena him. In his shame and despair Hecky commits suicide, but Howard is still not frightened. Unwilling to take a stand and decide whether to take the First or the Fifth Amendment or to cooperate, Howard decides to go before HUAC unprepared and try to "con" his way out. At first his evasions and pretended incomprehension seem to work, but soon he realizes that the committee knows about his illegal bookmaking activities, and he is forced to choose sides. He stands up and tells the panel of "re-spectable" gentlemen: "I'm sorry, but I don't recognize this Com-mittee's right to ask these kinds of questions. And you can all go fuck yourselves." After the last shot at Howard, handcuffed but with Florence by his side, Sinatra starts crooning again, "Fairy tales can come true . . ."

The ending of *The Front* is indeed a fairy tale. Although several people were indicted for contempt of court and imprisoned dur-ing the 1950s, nobody actually questioned the rights of HUAC as directly as Howard Prince does in this film. In terms of the movie as a whole, however, Sinatra's song is extremely ironic because *The Front* marks the Allen persona's final dissociation from the *shlemiel* figure.

The *shlemiel* character, as we have seen, is capable of keeping his faith in the most dire of circumstances. He is seen as the only morally sane man exactly because he remains young at heart no matter how cruelly the world treats him. McCarthyism does not, however, leave room for *shlemiels*. Thus, when Howard is young at heart, in this context he seems extremely "narrow of mind." Like Kleinman he does not want to get involved, but he finally has to realize that Alfred is right when he tells him, "You always think there's a middle you can dance around in, Howard. I'm telling you, there's no middle. And you can't lay this off on us. Whatever you do, you're doing it for yourself." In an era like the 1950s, in other words, one has no choice but to give up one's innocence and take a stand.

Finally, the stand that Howard has to take is not a political stand as much as a moral one. When Hecky Brown first goes to see Mr. Hennessy at the "Freedom Information Service," he is asked to name the names of other participants in a demonstration he was once involved in. When he pretends not to remember, Hennessy assures him that "They remember you!" thus revealing that he already knows who "they" are. It is not the information he is after—he knows the names already—but Hecky's cooperation.

The point of the interrogation is not what Hecky can tell HUAC, but what HUAC can make Hecky do to himself and his friends. Likewise when Howard has to go before the committee, they want to see how far he will go. Or, as Alfred predicts, "They don't care about names. They care about getting people to *give* names. They want to show there's nothing they can't get people to do."

At the beginning of *The Front,* Howard is at the same stage as Kleinman in "Death." He has already taken leave of his innocence and is a coward who does not want to become involved or take on a moral responsibility. By the end of the film, he has given up his "young at heart" attitude as well. If *The Front,* in the final analysis, is not a very subtle political or philosophical film, it does offer a number of insights into the McCarthy period which were slightly ahead of the great works on that era, such as Allen Weinstein's *Perjury* (1978) and Victor Navasky's *Naming Names* (1980). Most importantly in this connection, however, it marks a radical transformation in Allen's work, and for the subsequent half decade, Allen's persona will be characterized by suspicion, paranoia, and cynicism.

In her autobiographical account of the McCarthy period, *Scoundrel Time,* Lillian Hellman recounts an incident where Clifford Odet's vows to her that he will go before "those bastards on the Committee . . . and tell them to go fuck themselves."[27] Shortly afterward, when he does appear before HUAC, he testifies as a friendly witness and informs on several of his friends. Hellman is shocked and puzzled by his behavior and theorizes that moral conduct ought to be obvious from reactions in similar situations in childhood: "It's all been decided so long ago, when you are very young, all mixed up with your childhood definition of pride and dignity."[28]

One element that has changed in Allen's next movie, *Annie Hall,* is precisely the child figure. Heywood Allen, despite his being a "cocky kid," was constantly assaulted, and Virgil Starkwell even volunteered to step on his own glasses. When the early Allen persona was conning people, he did so not in front of them, but in front of us, the audience. He deflated them after they had left and he was out of danger. His was, to use an expression that Hellman applied to the 1950s, the "bravery of the staircase."[29] Alvy Singer, the central character in *Annie Hall,* also deflates his opponents directly to his audience, but he does so when they are present. Yet since they are usually intellectual rather than physical enemies, they are at a disadvantage, and are thus Alvy's victims rather than the other way around.

4

A Little Faith in People (1977–1979)

Old Man Sunshine—listen you!
Never tell me dreams come true!
Just try it—
And I'll start a riot.[1]
—Ira Gershwin, *But Not for Me*

Despite the considerable development in Woody Allen's films from *Take the Money and Run* to *Love and Death,* nothing in them quite prepares us for the extraordinary achievement of *Annie Hall.* After five films, which were all made from what Allen calls "secondary material"—not necessarily second-rate, but often secondhand, he moved 100 percent into the private sphere and the "much more subtle contemporary conflicts." The result is one of the funniest, most moving, and most memorable films about male/female relationships in film history.

During the filming of *The Front,* on December 1, 1975, Woody Allen turned forty. The central character and narrator of *Annie Hall,* Alvy Singer, is a Jewish stand-up comedian from New York who, just turned forty, is reconsidering his life with special emphasis on his relationship and break-up with Annie Hall. (Alvy is the first Allen character who has a distinctly Jewish name.)

In the opening scene, Alvy addresses the movie audience directly. He is standing strangely isolated against a cold background with no other sound than that of his own voice, and he tells us two jokes which reflect his apprehensions over life in general and relationships in particular. The first concerns two elderly ladies in the Catskills. One of them complains to the other that the food at the resort is terrible. The other one replies, "I know, and such small portions." And that, Alvy tells us, is more or less how he feels about life. "Full of loneliness and misery and suffering and unhappiness, and it's all over much too quickly." The second joke, which applies to Alvy's relationships with women, is usually, he tells us, attributed to Groucho Marx, "but I think it appears originally in Freud's *Wit and Its Relation to the Unconscious.* And it goes like this—I'm paraphrasing: 'I would never wanna belong to any club that would have someone like me for a member.' "

Alvy then proceeds to tell us that he and Annie broke up. "I keep sifting the pieces of the relationship through my mind," he says, in order to "figure out where did the screw-up come." He also tells us that he is "not a morose type. I'm not a depressive character. I was a reasonably happy kid, I guess. I was brought up in Brooklyn during World War 2."

What we see throughout the rest of the film is Alvy's "sifting" of the pieces. In stream-of-consciousness fashion we are presented with flashbacks of Alvy's recent as well as distant past. These not only contradict his assertion that he is not a "morose type" and had a happy childhood, but also indirectly explain what did go wrong with his and Annie's relationship. Thus, after the introduction, the scene shifts to Alvy's childhood in Brooklyn. He was brought up under the roller coaster in Coney Island, and in the first scene we see him, age nine, in a doctor's office. He is depressed and refuses to do his homework because he has read somewhere that "the universe is expanding." When Doctor Flicker looks at him uncomprehendingly, Alvy explains that "the universe is everything, and if it's expanding, someday it will break apart and that would be the end of everything!" Poor precocious Alvy does not get much support from his literal-minded but perhaps slightly more realistic mother: "What has the universe got do with it?" she shouts. "You're here in Brooklyn! Brooklyn is not expanding."

The adult Alvy Singer is equally disillusioned, misanthropic, paranoid, misunderstood, and anhedonic. (Anhedonia is a psychological term meaning the inability to experience pleasure.) He always, so his mother tells us, saw the worst in people. And whenever he is with his carefree and hedonistic friend Rob, he complains about the immorality and decay of the modern world, or of the increasing incidents of anti-Semitism—directed at himself: a friend of his said "not did you eat, but jew eat?" He is convinced that the rest of America regards New Yorkers as "left-wing Communist, Jewish, homosexual, pornographers. . . . I'm not discussing politics or economics. This is foreskin."

In the scene where we first see Annie, she is in a bad mood. Their relationship is already on the decline, and Alvy is irritated with her for not wanting to sleep with him and for talking too loud in public about their sexual problems. Yet, in the several flashbacks of their time together, we soon learn how delightfully different she is from depressive Alvy, and why he fell in love with her.

When they first meet, Alvy tries to impress her in a conversation on photography, which is Annie's new hobby: "Photography is interesting, 'cause, you know, it's a new art form, and a set of aesthetic criteria have not emerged yet. The medium enters in as a condition of the art form itself." The much less cerebral Annie, who clearly has no idea what Alvy is talking about, answers, "I just try to feel it, you know? I try to get a sense of it and not think about it so much." Likewise, when they go out to buy books together, Annie wants to buy a book about cats. Meanwhile Alvy want to buy her *Death and Western Thought* and *The Denial of Death* because, as he says, "I've a very pessimistic view of life. . . . I feel that life is divided up into the horrible and the miserable. . . . Those are the two categories."

Later when Annie is moving out of Alvy's apartment and they are dividing up their possessions, once more we see how their taste in books illustrates the differences between them. Annie says, "All the books on death and dying are yours and all the poetry books are mine." While Alvy is obsessed with death, Annie Hall is indeed a relievingly poetic and sanguine person who has an unusual capacity for merriment and optimism, and for transferring that optimism—at least for a while—to frustrated Alvy. While Annie too is neurotic, her neuroses manifest themselves not in depression and paranoia, but in a tendency to babble, make silly sounds, and occasionally laugh out of context. The most illuminating example of this is when, laughing hysterically, she tells a horrified Alvy the story of Grammy Hall's brother George, who suffered from narcolepsy and died while standing on line to get his free Christmas turkey from the union.

One problem with Annie and Alvy's relationship is that it is a version of the classic *shiksa* story: a Jewish man—often approaching middle age—falls in love with a young, beautiful, and relatively empty-headed WASP girl precisely because she is so very different from the world he grew up in. As soon as he manages to "get her," however, he tries to convert her so that she fits his world, to transform her into his mother—or in this case, himself. Thus no sooner is Alvy and Annie's relationship growing steady than Alvy wants her to become anhedonic, misanthropic, and obsessed with death, and he sends her to see a psychoanalyst. Despite all of Alvy's efforts, however, Annie persists in wanting to enjoy life, to be happy, and to smoke marihuana before making love. Ultimately Annie's insistence on holding on to her own carefree and babbling personality is what breaks up their relationship.

In *Love and Death*, Boris accounted for the village idiot's felicity by his very imbecility, his having nothing to worry about except "how much saliva to dribble." In *Annie Hall*, Alvy Singer turns this theory inside out. Not only is it easy to be happy if you are a half-wit, but being happy inevitably makes you one. Thus, when his relationship with Annie is beginning to dissolve, Alvy stops a young blissful looking couple in the street and asks them if they are in fact happy. When the woman confirms, Alvy wants to know how she accounts for that. "I'm very shallow and empty and I have nothing interesting to say," she volunteers, whereupon the man replies, "And I'm exactly the same way."

Alvy is even more suspicious of the possibility for and value of happiness than Boris was. His skepticism is revealed not only in his love affair with Annie, but also in his friendship with Rob. In *The Culture of Narcissism*, Lasch establishes a connection between the characteristics of the narcissistic personality type and certain general patterns in contemporary culture. Some of these characteristics clearly apply to the Allen persona. The most crucial of these would be his "nervous, self-deprecatory humor," "the intense fear of old age and death," "hypochondria," "fascination with oral sex," his "fear of the castrating mother,"[2] and "vague, diffuse dissatisfactions with life."[3]

As important, however, are the points where Alvy Singer, and the persona in most of Allen's subsequent films, dissociates from the narcissist. Quoting Jules Henry, Lasch argues that one important feature of the culture of narcissism is "the shift 'from a society in which the Super Ego values (the values of self-restraint) were ascendant to one in which more and more recognition was being given to the values of the id (the values of self-indulgence).'"[4] Self-indulgence clearly goes against the very grain of the Allen persona's character. He considers work the only valid form of expression and gets angry with his friends when they compromise their talent. When Annie feels attracted to the clean and laid-back life-style in California, Alvy tells her, "Yeah, and gradually you get old and die. You have to make a little effort once in a while!" Most importantly, Alvy is not only unable to enjoy himself, but is distracted and inhibited when other people do so, as is brilliantly illustrated in the early scene where as a child he is all but incapable of eating his *borscht* because hedonists are riding the roller coaster above his house.

His friend Rob, on the other hand, is presented as a superficial male-chauvinist imbecile who is lax with his work, and whose greatest interest in life is sleeping with seventeen-year-old twins who look like the women in *Playboy* magazine. When contrasting Alvy and Rob, it becomes clear that the former is more of a self-restrained moralist than a self-indulgent narcissist. In Allen's later work, we often find a male friend, like Rob, who functions as a counterbalance, so that the Allen persona's fears, phobias, and depressions seem more a reflection of his ethics than of egomania.

Allen illustrates this point even further by equating Alvy and New York City. Toward the end, Annie, who has now moved to California, tells him that he is incapable of enjoying himself and that, like Manhattan, he is an island. The city reflects Alvy and his obsessions; his paranoia, his misanthropy, his wide range of cultural interests, and his frantic, neurotic energy.

California, by contrast, represents everything he most abhors. He tells his friend Rob, who wants to move there, that he cannot live in a city whose only cultural advantage is the right to "make a right turn on a red light." During their Christmas trip to Los Angeles, Alvy is appalled by the inconsistent architecture and the "religious cult murders" and "wheat germ killers." Accordingly all the characters who are associated with California become decadent, and, because they are not obsessed with morality, morally corrupted in Alvy's eyes. The prime example of this is the record producer Tony Lacey (lazy?), for whom Annie eventually leaves Alvy. Lacey seems to be interested only in being "mellow," relaxed, and stoned, as do all the guests at his decadently elaborate Christmas party.[5]

When Rob has moved to California, he tells Alvy of his affair with the seventeen-year-old twins. Alvy reacts to Rob's shallowness and shows his despite for frivolity as well as his ensuing love for New York City by pointing out that, being an actor, Rob ought to be doing Shakespeare in the Park instead of fooling around. Rob's view of New York differs from Alvy's, though: He says, "I did Shakespeare in the Park, Max. I got mugged. I was playing Richard the Second and two guys with leather jackets stole my leotard." Nevertheless, to Alvy it is preferable to be industrious and intellectually aware, even if that may involve getting mugged and lead to anhedonia, than to be safe, comfortable, and have "nothing interesting to say," though that may involve happiness. Furthermore, Alvy does not regard the city as particularly dangerous; the country represents a much greater threat to him. As he says when his second wife wants to move there, "The country makes me nervous. [There are] crickets and . . . the Manson family . . . [and] Dick and Perry." (A reference to the two killers who wipe out an entire family in Truman Capote's novel *In Cold Blood*.)

The portrayal of Annie, who is anxious to achieve happiness, also changes as she begins to drift away from Alvy. Despite the genuine sympathy the film has shown for her up until that point, her moving out of Alvy's apartment and life is seen not as an indication of increased independence and endeavor, but rather as an unwillingness to "make an effort." During most of the film, Annie is seen as fresh, alert, and ready to develop. She understandably feels slightly suffocated by her relationship with dominating, regressive Alvy (as expressed in her dream where she castrates Frank Sinatra, who—according to her analyst—is a metaphor for Alvy Singer). But, by having her move to California rather than just away from Alvy, Allen suggests regress rather than progress for her. Her life in Los Angeles, as compared to that in New York, is so languid that it borders on inanity. As she explains to Alvy, "I meet people and I go to parties and we play tennis. I mean, that's a very big step for me."

It is indeed a big step from her life with Alvy, but what she achieves by moving out of their stifling relationship could hardly be called independence. Instead of going to bookstores, movies, and delicatessens with Alvy and staying home from parties because he wanted to, she now goes to Grammy Awards with Tony Lacey because *he* is nominated. Her own career as a singer, which she went to California to pursue, is significantly not mentioned with one word, indicating, of course, that nothing ever came of it. In terms of the morality of the film itself, Annie would have been much better off if she had stayed in New York and learned how to assert herself in that environment. Although Tony Lacey's pleasure dome may be an economic improvement, it certainly is not a personal one. For all her delusive self-confidence in the Beverly Hills scene, Annie Hall had a preeminent personal style and was a much more exciting and energetic woman when she was confused and agitated in disconcerting New York City. It should be noted, however, that at the end of the film Annie has moved back to New York and her old life style, as illustrated by her taking her new lover to see *The Sorrow and the Pity*.

Thus, it seems to me slightly facile when a number of critics agree that Annie and Alvy's break-up is not only necessary but positive because of the incongruity between them. It is precisely the fact that they are so different as to be almost antithetical that makes them compatible. The inimitable vitality between Woody Allen and Diane Keaton as actors and Alvy Singer and Annie Hall as lovers—which has appropriately led Garson Kanin to compare them to Tracy and Hepburn—is caused primarily by their dissimilarity. Whereas traditionally the dichotomy in comic duos is physical—short/tall, fat/thin, etc.—in this case it is psychological, which is in perfect accordance with the fact that Allen's natural domain is psychological rather than physical comedy.

On a couple of occasions, Allen visualizes the negative aspects of their dissimilarity by means of a split screen. In one instance Alvy is eating an Easter ham with the Hall family and assumes the appearance of a Hassidic Jew because the extremely anti-Semitic Grammy Hall keeps staring at him. Alvy starts thinking how different this gorgeous *goyishe* family is from his own. The two are, he tells us, like oil and water. Immediately the screen splits, and we see Alvy's family, bickering and shouting about death and disease over their *Pesach Seder*. Although the two families make an attempt at communicating across the split screen, they do not understand each other, and are completely incompatible. Later in the film, Allen uses the split screen to show the growing gap between Alvy and Annie. We see them in sessions with their respective analysts: Annie is in modern and progressive surroundings; Alvy is in a cluttered room that resembles Freud's study in Vienna, with Alvy lying down to visualize his regressiveness. Their respective analysts ask them how often they have sex. "Hardly ever," Alvy replies. "Maybe three times a week." Annie's answer to the question is "Constantly! I'd say three times a week." (In both instances, as Maurice Yacowar points out, Alvy takes up two-thirds of the split screen and Annie only one-third.)

The dissimilarity between the two of them, however, inspires a tremendous rapport that is illustrated in several scenes throughout the film. At the end of the movie, Alvy looks back at their great moments together and many of these scenes are repeated in a nostalgic collage: their walking along the dock when Alvy tells her he "lo-oves" her, the scene when they first talk in the tennis lobby, Alvy killing a spider in Annie's apartment, but most illuminatingly the lobster scene, which Alvy later tries to reenact with another woman. The incident of trying to get live lobsters into boiling water was clownish and delightful with Annie, while with the other date it falls flat. With Annie there was a lot of screaming and giggling quite atypical of Alvy, and the handheld camera emphasized the chaotic mood. With the other woman Alvy runs around hysterically trying to catch the stray lobsters, while she—like the camera—is stationary and detached.

Finally Alvy ends the movie as he opened it: with a joke. Annie has moved back to New York, and the two of them have had lunch and talked about old times. As they leave the café, the camera remains focused on the sadly empty street after they have walked out of the frame, and we hear Alvy in a voice-over, trying once more to relate his experiences in terms of an old joke. A man goes to a psychiatrist because his brother thinks he is a chicken. The doctor recommends that he turn his brother in, but that is not possible, the man says, because he needs the eggs. And that, Alvy tells us is "pretty much how I feel about relationships. You know, they're totally irrational and crazy and absurd . . . but I guess we keep going through it because most of us need the eggs."

In Woody Allen's early works, as we saw, there was a split between dream and reality. In *Annie Hall* that split is used again, but in a new and exhilarating way. At the beginning of the film, Alvy confesses that he has a hyperactive imagination. His mind tends to jump around, he tells us, "and I have some trouble between fantasy and reality." Throughout the movie, Allen's use of unusual technical and narrative devices supports this con- fession. The use of the split screen is one example. Another is the use of double exposure; to illustrate Annie's boredom, he has her get out of bed while Alvy is still making love to her. In one scene Allen uses a cartoon strip of Alvy, Rob, and Annie as the wicked queen in *Snow White*. When the three of them go to visit Alvy's old Brooklyn neighborhood, they watch and comment on incidents from his childhood. Finally, at one point when Annie and Alvy are standing on a movie-line in front of a pontificating Columbia University professor who irritates Alvy with his assertions about Fellini and Marshall McLuhan, Alvy pulls the latter out from behind a movie poster to tell the braggart that he does not know anything about McLuhan's theories. "How you ever got to teach a course in anything is totally amazing," McLuhan says. After which Alvy turns to his movie audience and says, "Boy, if life were only like this!" What is indicated, of course, is that life is not like that, and that Alvy, in contrast to the earlier Allen persona, does not believe that it is possible to deflate one's enemies in real life.

Surprisingly, enough, what these "flights of fancy" ultimately supply is not, as in the earlier films, a sharp contrast between fantasy and reality, but rather an extra dimension to reality. Thus, at the end of the film when Alvy is directing his new play, we are willing to accept the outer structure of the film as reality, and the substructure of the play as fantasy, or perhaps rather art. Whereas in "real life" Annie refused Alvy's marriage proposal, the play has a happy ending: Annie decides to go back to New York with him. Alvy then turns to the audience to explain that it was his first play and that one is "always trying to get things to come out perfect in art because it's real difficult in life." At this point we are so persuaded by the film that we do not immediately react to this distinction, but merely accept Alvy's manipulation and thus regard *Annie Hall* not as art and not as fantasy, but as real life.

At the end of *Love and Death,* Boris told the audience that he has learned that "human beings are divided into mind and body." The central dichotomy in Allen's work so far has been between the mind and the body, a dichotomy which could be seen as a reflection of the fantasy/reality distinction: the mind as the pursuer of fantasy and the body as the performer of reality. Also the two forms of humor used in these works, slapstick and verbal, are closely connected with this division: slapstick as the comedy of the body and verbal humor as that of the intellect. Likewise the basic situation of the Allen persona in the three films, *Bananas, Sleeper,* and *Love and Death,* is rooted in this dichotomy. Because the *shlemiel* is physically weak and placed in a hostile environment which threatens his body, he is forced to rely entirely on his oral rapidity and the ingenuity of his wits in order to escape.

In *Annie Hall* and most of Allen's subsequent films, the emphasis has shifted. The Allen persona is no longer displaced, but right in the middle of his natural habitat, New York City. In *Stardust Memories* (1980), the central character Sandy Bates says about Vittorio de Sica's *The Bicycle Thief:* "Obviously if you don't have enough to eat, or something, that becomes a major problem. . . . But what happens if you're living in a more, you know, uh, a more affluent society, and you're lucky enough to—to not have to worry about *that?*" Unlike Virgil Starkwell, Alvy Singer and his successors all live in "affluent" environments. Their concerns are the "contemporary conflicts" discussed in the previous chapter, that is, the culture of narcissism. They are in no immediate physical danger. Even though the universe may be expanding, to them the "body" part of the earlier dichotomy is of no real interest, and, accordingly, the slapstick gradually disappears from Allen's films. The main preoccupation of the movies made after *The Front* has to do with moral principles and ethics. The central dichotomy is between the heart and the brain, the emotional and the intellectual.[6]

In *Annie Hall,* as in all of Allen's films, the attitude toward intellectuals is ambivalent. When Alvy goes to a party with his second wife and the people from *Dysentery* (he has heard that *Commentary* and *Dissent* have merged and formed *Dysentery*), Alvy says that his wife's friends prove that it is possible to be "absolutely brilliant" and at the same time have "no idea what's going on."

Despite his distaste for intellectualism, however, Alvy represents the brain in *Annie Hall.* In fact, his brain is his main problem. It is his awareness of death and the expanding universe which makes him incapable of anything but momentary release and happiness. Annie, on the other hand, very much represents the heart. Her intelligence is native and not cerebral. At times, in fact, one tends to wonder whether she has a full deck at her disposal. Or, as Woody Allen said about Diane Keaton, "When I first met her, her mind was a complete blank."[7] Annie Hall is a disarmingly carefree person with a tremendous gift for poetry and laughter who generally tries to "get a sense of it and not think about it so much."

There is an old Yiddish proverb that says: "If you put your brain before your heart, you're a king. If you put your heart before your brain, you're a fool." Although the Yiddish tradition is a highly cerebral one, it has always preferred fools to kings, and Annie Hall is in fact the "fool" and *shlemiel* of this movie. In *Play It Again, Sam!, Sleeper,* and *Love and Death,* the Diane Keaton figure played alongside the Allen persona and shared his *shlemiel* status with him; in this film she takes over that role almost entirely. Where the Allen character has developed into an austere and anhedonic character, she represents the innocent, "young at heart" attitude which the Allen persona lost in connection with *The Front.* Although it may sound strange that this extremely WASP character, whose family is incompatible with Alvy's Jewish family, should function as the typically Yiddish *shlemiel,* it becomes less inconceivable in the context of Allen's work and his universalizing of the Jewish figure discussed in the first chapter. Indeed, in a number of Allen's later films, the resilient and mirth-loving characteristics of the *shlemiel* have likewise been taken over by non-Jewish characters.

There is one other factor that distinguishes the films discussed in this and the following chapters from those in the previous chapter—a factor which is connected with the mind/body and heart/brain dichotomies. In the earlier films where the Allen persona was displaced, the threat was an external one. In the later films, the conflicts are highly internal. In the earlier films the danger was in the environment; in the later ones the danger is within the Allen persona himself. It is not so much the *fact* that the universe is expanding and that we are all going to die which is perilous to him as it is his own awareness of that fact. It is not reality that is dangerous but the Allen persona's imagination and what it can make of reality. In fact, the universe may be expanding, but "Brooklyn," as Alvy's quite sensible although not very sensitive mother says, "*is not* expanding."

Both the external struggle in the earlier films and the internal struggle in the later ones are reflected in the setting. Where *Bananas, Sleeper,* and *Love and Death* are all filmed almost entirely in exteriors, the films discussed in this chapter take place primarily in interior settings. And, because they are set in Allen's natural surroundings, New York City, even the exterior scenes seem interior in that the environment is not threatening to the Allen character. As Woody Allen himself said, "cities are more civilized, more controlled," almost as controlled, in fact, as living rooms.[8] As if to illustrate my point, Allen was kind enough to actually name his next film *Interiors.*

Unlike Charles Chaplin who always saw comedy as an art-form in its own right, Woody Allen has on several occasions diminished the value of his comic work. To his biographer Eric Lax he said:

> There is no question in my mind that comedy is less valuable than serious stuff. It has less of an impact, and I think for a good reason. When comedy approaches a problem, it kids it but it doesn't resolve it. Drama works it through in a more emotionally fulfilling way.[9]

Making comedies rather than "serious" films was to Allen like "sitting at the children's table." *Interiors* is clearly his attempt to advance to the table of the grownups. Possibly he did not realize that he had already done so with his depictions of the "contemporary conflicts" in *Annie Hall.*

The audiences who, in their enthusiasm over Allen's previous film and its five Academy Awards, flocked to see *Interiors* were in for a somewhat unpleasant surprise. It turned out not to be a comedy, but a modern family drama, thematically derived from Chekhov, Ibsen, Strindberg, and O'Neill, and cinematically inspired by the films of Ingmar Bergman. This time Allen's models were not parodied as in his earlier works, but seriously emulated.

The film opens with a series of still life shots of the two sisters, Joey and Renata, and the family's beach house. In the next scene, Arthur, a middle-aged, middle-class, gentile man tells us that he

decided to leave his successful, dominating interior decorator wife
Eve because the rigid harmony she created around her family
stifled him. Although most of the dialogue of this film is con-
ducted by Joey and Renata, we soon learn that it is centered on
Eve, her neuroses and the effect she has on her family.

The plot of the film, which is not presented chronologically,
stretches from the time when Arthur tells his family about his
decision to leave them until Eve's self-inflicted death approximately a month later. We follow the family through a period of
hope of a reunion for Eve, of remarrying for Arthur, and of
oedipal conflicts and sibling rivalry between two of the three
grown-up daughters.

Renata, the oldest daughter, is a successful poet whose relationship with her mother is relatively conflictless and marked with
a feeling of mutual respect for each other's art and perfectionism.
But, exactly because she is so much like her mother, Renata enters
a traumatic period in her life when she realizes that she is "not
very far from the age when my mother began showing signs of
strain." In effect she *is* her mother, and just like Eve's family has
felt stifled by her fastidiousness, so Renata's husband—*her* family—is stifled and unmanned by her creativity.

Younger sister Joey envies Renata's professional success and her
relationship with their mother; she is, in turn, envied by Renata
for her closer relationship with Arthur. At a visit to Eve in a
sanatorium after an attempted suicide, Renata accuses Joey of
feeling guilty toward her mother and therefore obligated to spend
more time with her than the other sisters. With a great Freudian
blunder, Joey proves that Renata is right: "I—I don't believe this.
My whole life I've only wanted to *be* her." Even though she
practically succeeds at "being" Eve in terms of her relationship
with her father, Joey cannot live up to her mother professionally.
She has, as Renata says, all the "anguish and anxiety" of an artist
but, despite frantic attempts at finding her metier, none of the
talent.

The youngest sister only appears sporadically. Flyn is a
modestly successful television actress, and partly because she
travels so much, the outsider of the family. Although on the
surface she seems to be empty-headed and self-centered—"a perfect example," Renata's husband Frederik says, "of form without
any content,"—she turns out to be the most honest and least
sterile of the three. She is the only one who openly dares deal with
her failure: "If it wasn't for the stupid television industry I

wouldn't make enough to live. . . . I have a few good years, then . . . my youth will be frozen on old celluloid."

Joey's friend Mike is by far the warmest, most flexible, and unneurotic character we meet in the first half of the film. He is the only one who has the energy to be concerned with other people and their problems. Not only is he, on a personal level, extremely supportive and understanding toward Joey, but in his work he shows a social and political awareness for which Joey and her family, as she says, are "too self-centered." Mike is a contrast to all the cerebral characters in the film in that he is sincerely preoccupied with moral issues which they can only consider intellectually. In the first scene after Arthur's monologue, Mike is alone. Speaking into a tape recorder, he suddenly says—out of context and much to his own surprise: "The hardest thing is to act properly throughout one's whole life."

Strangely enough, we know hardly anything about Arthur despite the fact that he opened the film, and appropriately he did have his back to the camera. He is an extremely bland character who seems to have no will of his own, and it is not hard to believe that he would feel threatened by as competent and dominating a woman as his first wife. He is, Renata tells her analyst, Eve's "creation." "She put him through law school and she financed the start of his practice." His past, then, seems to have been determined by a demanding, strong-willed, and difficult woman, and his future, as far as we can see, is about to be determined by a more flexible and warmhearted one.

Toward the middle of the film, Arthur brings his new lady friend to meet his daughters. Pearl is as different from Eve and her world as is possibly imaginable, and the two sisters are embarassed by her uncouth straightforwardness. Where Eve wears "ice-grey," Pearl breaks out of Eve's interior decorating with her red dress. She is loud and frank, loves her steaks "blood-rare," and on her travels prefers beaches, sand, and dancing to cathedrals and ruins. For Pearl the main thing is not to create no matter what the price, but to enjoy and use the one life you have. As she says to the bewilderment of the sisters, and with food in her mouth, "You only live once. But once is enough if you play it right." Later, when Arthur refuses another piece of cheesecake, Pearl says, "You'll live to be a hundred if you give up all the things that make you want to."

In her liveliness and sanguinity Pearl seems to come from another planet than the anemic, neurotic sisters. Her sense of morality is as shocking to them as her ravenous appetite for life.

When discussing a play they have seen, Renata finds it necessary in her argument to evoke Socrates, Buddha, Schopenhauer, and Ecclesiastes, while Frederik and Joey discuss the difficulty of taking a moral stand. Pearl, with the simplicity and unaffectedness of the *shlemiel*, has less trouble: "It wasn't such a big deal. One guy was a squealer, the other guy wasn't. I liked the guy that wasn't." Her moral dictum is simply: "You just don't squeal." In addition to considering the intellectual values of the play, Mike is the only one capable of being "very moved" by it.

When, on Arthur and Pearl's wedding night, Eve suddenly appears unexpectedly and drowns herself, Joey demonstrates a resolution and courage we did not know she has when she runs after her mother to save her and nearly gets killed in the process. Significantly, the only two people who are awake to help Joey are Mike and Pearl. Mike rescues her, and Pearl brings her back to life with mouth-to-mouth resuscitation, literally blowing life into her. At Eve's funeral Joey seems to have come to terms with herself. She is composed and finally capable of reconciling with Renata, her former competitor. After the funeral service she even sits down to write: "I felt compelled to write these thoughts down. They seemed very powerful to me."

Presumably Joey's inhibition and the animosity she felt toward Renata are gone with her demanding and dominating mother. All the anguish and frustration of the sisters, so they tell us, were caused by their relationship with Eve, and after her death, the sea which destroyed her is "calm" and "peaceful." Though the stifling and villainous mother figure is by no means a new phenomenon in American culture—recent examples would be Sophie Portnoy in literature and Mary Tyler Moore in *Ordinary People* in film—in Allen's film Eve is used in a slightly more subtle and ambiguous fashion.

In Ingmar Bergman's 1978 film, *Autumn Sonata*, we find a similar theme: a talented and successful artist mother is accused by her older daughter of being responsible for her own emotional as well as her sister's physical disablement. In a review by Vernon Young the validity of these accusations is questioned. It is, as Young points out, "possible to take the other view, that Bergman intended the Liv Ullman [sic] character to reveal herself unmistakenly as a self-pitying neurotic, whose charges are patently canceled by the clearly delineated superiority of the mother."[10] Likewise, if we accept Eve as "guilty" of her family's accusations and her husband and daughters as the martyrs they seem to think they are, Allen's movie seems extremely schematic and predictable. But the fact is that no matter how convincingly her family deprecates her, it is difficult to believe that the woman we see, for all her manipulativeness, could indeed be responsible for so many messed-up lives. Finally, one cannot help but feel a little sorry for her.

The Eve we see throughout the film is but a shadow of the successful and self-assured person that her family tells us about. Despite everyone's assumption that the separation was the cause of her breakdown, we are told that she has been in and out of sanatoriums for many years, and that Arthur had had several affairs in the meantime. In fact, as Renata tells her analyst, Eve was not much older than Renata is now when she "began showing signs of strain." Although it is obvious to the observant spectator that underneath her famous cool facade Eve is falling apart, her family keeps reassuring themselves and each other that she is doing "much better than we all expected." Arthur and her daughters refuse to talk with her or even listen to her worries. Renata patronizes her, and Joey discourages her, but throughout the film they are both more concerned with their own narcissistic sibling rivalry. Ultimately, Eve, and not her daughters and husband, is the victim of this movie because nobody really cares about her. Although her family seems to think that this film is "all about Eve," it is practically not about Eve at all.

When they visit Eve after her attempted suicide, Arthur and Renata end up fighting because Arthur, as Renata says, is "obsessed with Joey while mother is lying in a hospital room." It is clear, however, that what Renata is expressing is not so much concern for her mother as oedipal jealousy. The selfishness of this conversation seems even more striking than similar scenes in the film because of the brilliantly shot preceding scene of Eve preparing her suicide. The camera is focused on a close up of her hands putting black tape on the windows of her beautiful but lonely apartment. When she runs out of tape, the camera remains frozen on the window until her hands return with more tape. This absurd and slightly embarrassing triviality of running out of tape in the face of death is a serious parallel to the deflating death jokes in *Without Feathers* and *Love and Death,* and this is indeed one of the most powerful scenes in the film.

Finally, what the movie is negative toward is not so much Eve herself as her values, which happen to be Renata and Joey's values as well. In *Interiors,* as in all Woody Allen's work, there is an anti-intellectual strain that is personified in Pearl. Where Eve's world with its perfectionist artistic view and exaggerated emphasis on creativity is seen as cold and sterile, Pearl's spontaneous, loving, noncerebral (although slightly "low-brow") world is seen as warm and exuberant.

Strangely enough, the most serious flaw of Allen's first non-comic film is its cluttered language. What might have been expressed through images alone, is often explained with too many unnecessary words, which, at times, sound embarassingly "intel-lectual." The verbal pseudo-intellectualism goes against the grain of the movie itself, and despite the fact that in comedy Woody Allen realizes that his strength lay in verbal and not visual humor, the best scenes in *Interiors* are the purely visual ones: the opening still life shots, Eve's attempted suicide, and Renata's anxiety attack when she is trying to write.

When critics have argued that *Interiors* is nothing but a bad imitation of Bergman, that this clown wanted to play not the prince of Denmark, but the "king of Swedish filmmakers," I think they are being more than slightly unreasonable.[11] James Monaco moaned: "We have depended on Allen for more than ten years now as a champion against just this particular sort of bad-faith artiness and the mid-cult sensibility from which it stems."[12] In their childish, sulking disappointment these critics refused to deal with Allen's attempt at noncomic film in a serious manner.

The fact that *Interiors* is not as artistically successful as *Annie Hall* or as haunting as Ingmar Bergman's films is less important than Allen's willingness to risk his popularity for the sake of broaden-ing his mind by refusing to give people what they expected of him. What he once said of Chaplin, in this case applies to himself: "What happens with a more serious artist, like Chaplin, is you try to do other things. You don't go to your strength all the time. And you strike out so people think you're an ass or pretentious, but that's the only thing you can do."[13] Whatever one thinks of *Inte-riors,* there can be no doubt that it contributed significantly to Allen's skills as a director and to the uniqueness of a number of his subsequent films, most immediately *Manhattan,* which was re-leased the following year, in 1979.

To the great relief of his audience, Allen had once again re-turned to comedy, although a slightly different kind. In *Manhat-tan,* Allen successfully combines the bittersweet humor that we glimpsed in *Annie Hall* with the philosophical and moral issues that he had been fascinated by ever since *Love and Death,* along with the visual skills that he had acquired during the filming of *Interiors.*

Like *Annie Hall* and *Interiors, Manhattan* is set in New York, but this time the city takes on a metaphoric, almost fabled, quality. Allen's mythologizing of his city is emphasized by the Gershwin songs, the lyrics of which are used very precisely to correspond to the plot, and by Gordon Willis's superb photography. *Manhattan* is filmed in black and white, rather than the bright colors one normally sees in the typical New York film of the last two or three decades. Likewise, the great variety of buildings and landmarks presented to us in the opening scene to the accompaniment of *Rhapsody in Blue* are, rather surprisingly, covered with snow. By the time Isaac Davis, the central character of the film, finishes his voice-over interpretations of the city (New York as a jungle, New York as a metaphor for the decay of contemporary culture, etc.), and we see the last shots of the Manhattan skyline and fireworks, still amazingly shot in black and white, New York City seems slightly unreal and extremely nostalgic.

Ultimately, this understated, nonrealistic setting allows us to concentrate on the characters, who are in turn closer to real life than even Alvy Singer. Isaac Davis smokes without choking, drinks without trying to take his pants off over his head, and manages to drive a car without wrecking it. Like *Annie Hall*, *Manhattan* is a film about interhuman relationships: male/female relationships as well as friendships. What is portrayed here, however, is not so much the mechanisms—how relationships form, fade, and dissolve—as the moral implications, responsibilities, and potential fulfillment they involve. Where Alvy was inhibited by his obsessions with morality, mortality, and the universe, and Renata sterilized by hers, Isaac eventually is enabled to grow through his.

Isaac Davis has two broken marriages and a child behind him. His second wife, Jill, left him for another woman and is presently writing a revealing book about their marriage and divorce.[14] At the beginning of the film, Isaac is involved with beautiful, sensitive seventeen-year-old Tracy. His best friend Yale is, or so he insists, happily married to Emily, but involved with highly neurotic Mary Wilke. As both Yale and Mary feel guilty about their affair, Yale decides to break up, and he pushes Mary over to Ike, whom he knows feels slightly ashamed over Tracy because of her age. Both Yale and Mary change their minds, however, and leave Emily and Ike respectively. Ike gets furious and realizes that he made a mistake when he gave up Tracy. When he finally contacts her to ask her to come back, she is on her way to London on a scholarship. She asks him to wait for her for six months: "Well, I mean, what's six months if we still love each other. . . . Not everybody gets corrupted. Look, you have to have a little faith in people."

After the opening montage, we are introduced to *Elaine's,* Yale, Ike, Emily, Tracy, and the central concern of the movie—in that order. Ike wants to know what would happen if on the way home they saw a person drowning in The East River. Would any one of them be brave enough to jump in and save him? Ike says that to him "Talent is luck. I think the important thing in life is courage." Parallel to the divisions in *Annie Hall* and *Interiors,* the characters in this film are indeed divided into those who have talent— brains—and those who have courage—heart.

At the beginning of the film, Isaac, like the earlier Allen persona, is a coward morally, as we see when he says that the dilemma he himself presented is not relevant to him because he cannot swim, and physically, as we see in a scene a little later when he gets an anxiety attack because a thunderstorm breaks out during his walk in Central Park with Mary. There is not much left of the *shlemiel.* His moral and philosophical simplicity is gone, as is his acute sense of survival. Instead, as in the two previous films, these components of the *shlemiel* role are taken over by another character, namely, the young girl Tracy. Considering how completely antithetical the Hemingway hero is to everything the *shlemiel* stands for, it seems ironic that Allen should have chosen Ernest Hemingway's granddaughter—although she is perfect for the role—to represent that character in his film. Wisse defines a *shlemiel* as somebody who refuses to resign and say "Yes. Isn't it pretty to think so" (the closing remark in Hemingway's *The Sun Also Rises*).[15] Like Annie and Pearl, Tracy represents the sensitive, common sense, morally intact mentality. She is the one who has the honesty and courage that the other characters lack. Faith, as we have seen, is one of the basic characteristics of the *shlemiel,* and Tracy's last words call to mind an old Yiddish tale, *A Mayse mit a Khokhm un a Tam,* in which the *shlemiel,* because of his simplicity and confidence, ends up a much admired and genial man, whereas his intelligent and skeptical friend experiences only poverty, dissatisfaction, and anxiety. Tracy, although she is by no means *tam* (stupid), is indeed a sharp contrast to all the neurotic intellectuals with their constant anxiety attacks.

Mary is unequivocally the embodiment of the opposite end of the spectrum. She is, as Isaac says to Tracy at the beginning of the film, "all cerebral." During one of her outings with him, Mary brags that she has got "a million facts on my fingertips," a rather childish "intellectual" achievement, it would seem. Like the *khokhm* (wise one) she is very familiar with anxiety and dissatisfaction; her life is a complete mess and she continually repeats that she wants to "straighten my life out." When she is with Yale, she keeps insisting that she deserves better than to be with a married man, and when she is with Isaac in bed, she admits that she was "faking a little bit," revealing the lack of honesty which makes her such a striking contrast to Tracy. Mary's confused and rather endearing irresponsibility is seen throughout the film, but most markedly at the end when Yale leaves his wife, and she is not sure whether her relationship with Yale is going to last more than the four weeks that Ike predicts because, as she tells him, "I can't plan that far in advance."

As opposed to Yale, however, Mary is at least doing what she believes is right. She is "from Philadelphia" where apparently you do not talk behind people's backs or break up their marriages. Her reluctance to let Yale divorce Emily in the first place is due to her own confused sense of what is morally right. Yale, on the other hand, wants to have his cake and eat it: stay with Emily and keep Mary (which is not good at all in Allen's book of moral codes). He wants his life to be as easy and painless as possible, and therefore lies to and betrays his wife, his mistress, and his best friend. He neglects his work and is generally unwilling to "make an effort." Where Mary is often sweet in her completely confused helplessness, Yale is a very contemptible character in the context of the film, or as Ike tells him when he finds out that Yale has been seeing Mary behind his back:

> You're too easy on yourself, don't you see that? That's your problem, that's your whole problem. You—you rationalize everything. You're not honest with yourself. You talk about you wanna write a book, but in the end, you'd rather buy the Porsche, you know, or you cheat a little bit on Emily, and you play around the truth a little with me, and the next think you know, you're in front of a Senate committee and you're naming names! You're informing on your friends.

Between young Tracy, who has complete personal integrity, and Mary and Yale who lack it entirely, we have Isaac. Like the Allen persona in *Love and Death* and *Annie Hall*, Ike is extremely preoccupied with his own mortality, and because he wants to be "well thought of" by posterity, he tries to achieve moral integrity, not altogether successfully.

In *Manhattan*, as in *Annie Hall* and later in *Stardust Memories*, the importance of a relationship is easily interpreted by the things the lovers do together. The Allen persona, and most markedly Ike Davis, has a clear definition of things that are worth doing and things that are not. Thus at the end of *Manhattan*, we see him lying on his couch, reciting the things that for him make life worth living. Among them are Groucho Marx, Mozart's *Jupiter Symphony*, Frank Sinatra, and the crabs at Sam Wo's. Mary and Yale, typically, have a negative equivalent to Isaac's list. Their "Academy of the Overrated" consists of geniuses and near-geniuses such as Gustav Mahler, Scott Fitzgerald, Lenny Bruce, and Walt Whitman, among others.

Yale and Mary spend most of the time we see them together bickering over their relationship, which obviously is not working for either of them as long as Yale is married. What seems to be most characteristic for them is that, very significantly, they continually have tickets to concerts which for one reason or another, they never seem to attend. Their plans never materialize.

In their brief relationship, Isaac and Mary seem to do very nice things together. Often, however, these things are slightly antithetical to Isaac's character. They go to the country, where the outer threats recall the early Allen movies. Big city person that he is, Ike finds that mosquitoes have "sucked all the blood out of my left leg." When they take a rowboat together on the Central Park lake, Ike romantically puts his hand in the water only to find it completely covered with mud and pollution when he pulls it up. Although they seem relatively relaxed together, Mary admits to having faked in bed because she is "a little nervous" around Ike.

All in all, there is no doubt that on the basis of the Allen persona's standards, Isaac and Tracy have the best and most interesting relationship. They go to museums, eat Chinese food in bed, and watch The Late Show W. C. Fields film on television.

Despite Ike's continual frustrations and complaints, they are very comfortable together and genuinely fond of each other. Unfortunately, Ike has trouble admitting this. He accuses Yale of not being honest with himself, but does not seem to realize that he is not honest with himself either when he gives up Tracy for Mary. Also, where betraying one's friends is concerned, he is not spotless, Tracy is clearly his most devoted friend, but he refuses to take her seriously solely because of her age. He later realizes his mistake and tells Emily:

> "I think of all the women I've known over the last years, when I actually am honest with myself, I think I had the most relaxed times and the most, you know, the nicest times with her. She was really a terrific kid, but young, right? . . . I really kept her at a distance and I would just never give her a chance."

He jokes a lot at Tracy's expense, and in the scene when he breaks up with her, he tells her not to cry because that makes her look like "one of those barefoot kids from Bolivia who need foster parents." Tracy, despite Ike's malicious irony, definitely does not need "foster parents," and it is interesting that it is, in fact, the older, more intellectually aware woman, Mary, who is portrayed as the helpless one.

All through the film we are reminded of Ike's moral frailty through the book his ex-wife is writing about their marriage. He is ludicrously scared of what she might say about him. When the book is finally published, it is indeed not flattering, although undoubtedly true. In fact, the only nice thing Jill can remember about Ike is that he cries every time he sees *Gone with the Wind*. Her description of him very precisely, but completely humorlessly, captures the Allen persona of this period: "He was given to fits of rage, Jewish, liberal paranoia, male chauvinism, self-righteous misanthropy, and nihilistic moods of despair. He had complaints about life but never any solutions." Although again the descriptions of the modern narcissist are even more true of the Allen persona's male friend, in this case Yale, they also do have some relevance for Isaac. Just how much, we see in the last scene of the film.

After an epiphanic scene in which Isaac discovers that "Tracy's face" is among the things that for him make "life worth living," he runs over to her house to ask her to come back to him. All through the film, the Gershwin songs are used to explain the characters and their relationships. When Ike is with confused and vulnerable Mary, we hear *Embraceable You* and *Someone to Watch over Me* and when he is with Tracy, who in many ways is more of an equal, the tunes are *He Loves and She Loves* and *Love Is Here to Stay*. The tune we hear just before Isaac diffidently faces Tracy in the last scene is *But Not For Me*.

Ike, so he tells Emily, is a "noncompromiser," so he immaturely still expects Tracy to do all the compromising a relationship would require. He thus asks her to give up her trip to London because he has changed his mind. He asks her to abandon her integrity to satisfy his whims. In accordance with her behavior throughout the film, Tracy refuses to act inauthentically and irresponsibly even for Ike's sake, and instead asks *him* to "make an effort" and wait for her for six months, in return promising that she will in fact come back to him. Isaac, hopefully, has learned his lesson. It is not enough to be obsessed with high moral standards about making an effort, not betraying your friends, and being too easy on yourself—you have to act on your convictions as well. It is up to us and our conception of the Allen persona to form our own personal opinion as to whether or not he has changed and decides to wait for Tracy.

Everything we know about Tracy tells us that she is right in assuming that she will not get "corrupted" during her stay in London, and that we can trust her promise. The Gershwin song thus reflects Isaac's self-pity rather than any realistic future. Tracy's last words, "Look, you have to have a little faith in people," give Isaac the chance to prove whether he himself possesses the "personal integrity" he accuses Yale and Mary of lacking. Whether or not "they are playing songs of love" for Isaac is now completely up to him.

5
Stardust (1980–1982)

When enough time has passed, events blur, facts fade, and
memories overtake reality. What we remember most vividly
becomes for each of us our version of the truth.[1]
—Richard Pells

In Allen's next two works, both of which came out in 1980—a
book of essays, *Side Effects*, and a movie, *Stardust Memories*—the
central themes are still the "contemporary conflicts" that were
portrayed in *Annie Hall, Interiors,* and *Manhattan.* Now, however,
these conflicts are carried to an extreme and the Allen persona
has become abnormally pessimistic.

Side Effects, like Allen's other books, closely corresponds to his
films. *Getting Even,* like the early films, was a hilarious, but slightly
immature work which was highly original despite its many invocations of Allen's predecessors. Its title reflected the tendency of the
Allen persona to solve his problems by deflating his enemies.
Without Feathers, like the middle films, was much more competent
stylistically, and the philosophy contained in the title was immediately and bathetically undermined. In *Side Effects*, Allen shows
an almost fully formed literary sensibility. Although we can still
detect traces of S. J. Perelman's narrative voice, *Side Effects*, like
the later movies, is a very original work whose main concern is no
longer to parody other artists and genres or even to be funny.

Like *Annie Hall* and *Manhattan, Side Effects* and *Stardust Memories*
are permeated with speculations on morality, death, the expanding universe, and male/female relationships which do not work.
They do not, however, claim to be in any way realistic. The essays
in this volume and the plot of *Stardust Memories* are not depictions
of these obsessions, but rather of their "side effects"; they are
delusions of a brain overwrought by them. "We must plunge into
experience and then reflect on the meaning of it," Johann Wolf-
gang Goethe said. "All reflection and no plunging drives us mad;

all plunging and no reflection and we are brutes."[2] All through Allen's work his persona has criticized "plunging," narcissistic imbeciles. At this point, however, it almost seems that his massive "reflection" over their immorality has driven him mad. Thus the reality that was charmingly distorted in *Annie Hall* has become grotesque in *Stardust Memories*. The congenial self-pity of Alvy Singer borders on egomania in Sandy Bates, the Allen persona in *Stardust Memories*. The conflict between dream and reality in Allen's work has turned into a conflict between nightmare and reality.

In *Take the Money and Run!*, Virgil's psychiatrist said that his relationship with Louise was the "healthiest thing in his life." In *Bananas* and *Sleeper,* personal relationships were seen as the solution to the problems that politics could not handle. In *Annie Hall,* Alvy experienced temporary release through his encounter with Annie and acknowledged that even if relationships are absurd, "most of us need the eggs." Even *Manhattan* ended on an optimistic note: it was up to Ike to make the effort if he wanted Tracy back. In *Side Effects* there is no such hope. Any relationship, no matter with whom, is bound to go wrong. One is reminded of what Miles said about *politics* at the end of *Sleeper:* "It does not matter who's up there. They're all terrible."

Thus in "The Shallowest Man," Lenny Mandel finds and gets the woman of his dreams but their relationship lasts only a year. In "The Lunatic's Tale," Dr. Ossip Parkis is involved with two women: one is pretty, kind, attractive, competent, and intelligent, but does not turn him on sexually; the other is voluptuous, but her intellectual capacity is limited to "est, alpha waves, and the ability of leprechauns to locate gold."[3] Being an excellent surgeon, Parkis decides to switch their brains around so as to create the perfect woman. After only a couple of months of marital bliss, he tires of her as well, possibly because nothing in nature is "actually 'perfect' with the exception of my Uncle Hyman's stupidity."[4]

More likely the Allen persona himself and his attitude toward relationships is to blame. Otto Rank once described the modern relationship as "hopelessly confused," because "one person is made godlike judge over good and bad in the other person. In the long run, such symbiotic relationships become demoralizing to both parties, for it is just as unbearable to be God as it is to remain an utter slave."[5] With Annie as well as Mary and Tracy, the Allen persona considered himself superior, recommending adult education for Annie, a change of psychoanalyst for Mary, and for Tracy to forget him and go and play with "Billy and Biff and

Scooter and, you know, little Tommy or Terry." And Ossip Parkis, of course, plays the ultimate God-figure and starts recreating human beings.

All through Allen's films of this period, his persona takes on the role of "godlike judge over good and bad" in his friends, family, and lovers. Toward the end of *Manhattan* when Ike starts moralizing over Yale's life, Yale screams at him: "You're so self-righteous, you know. You think you're God!" Ike accepts Yale's statement and replies: "I gotta model myself after someone!" Whereas the Allen persona constantly accuses his narcissistic friends of demanding too little of themselves, he himself could be accused of demanding too much of himself, and certainly of his friends and lovers. But as Ernst Becker said of modern relationships in *The Denial of Death*—the very book that Alvy insisted on buying for Annie Hall: "To want too little from the love object is as self-defeating as to want too much."[6]

For the Allen persona at this point, a lasting relationship is indeed not possible. Even in "The Kugelmass Episode" (which won an O'Henry Award in 1977), in which Sidney Kugelmass, professor of humanities at City College, can be projected into any novel of his choice by means of a magic box, his romance turns sour. Not only is it impossible for even Emma Bovary to meet his standards, but at the end of the story when he wants to be projected into *Portnoy's Complaint* so that he can meet "The Monkey," he is by mistake projected irrevocably into a Spanish grammar book instead, and thus literally trapped by his fantasy.

Finally, "Retribution," which ends the volume, is the most absurd, and also the most convincing story Allen has ever written. A setting is established which is reminiscent of the Easter scene in *Annie Hall*. The plot, however, takes a completely different and crooked turn. Harold Cohen comes from a family that is constantly "bickering over the best way to combat indigestion or how far back to sit from the television set." His parents have been married for forty years "out of spite." Connie Chasen's parents "hug and [drink] in lovey-dovey fashion," and think that Jews are "truly exotic." Connie's mother probably looks like Colleen Dewhurst (who played Annie's mother in *Annie Hall*): "fifty-five, buxom, tanned, a ravishing pioneer face with pulled-back greying hair and round, succulent curves."[7] Harold Cohen falls in love with Connie's mother but manages to control himself and establish a warm friendship with her. Connie cannot sleep with Harold because, now that he is so close with her mother, he reminds her of her brother, and Harold and Connie finally break up. The happy Chasens get a divorce: "My parents fight like the Montagues and Capulets and stay together their whole lives. Connie's folks sip martinis and hug with true civility and, bingo, they're divorced."[8] Harold and Connie's mother get married. At the wedding Connie tells Harold that now that he is her "father" and not her "brother" she wants to sleep with him again. Harold's conclusion to the story and thus to the book marks his final resignation: "All I could mutter to myself as I remained a limp, hunched figure was an age-old line of my grandfather's which goes 'Oy vey.'"[9]

If the stories in *Side Effects* are exaggerated and absurd, *Stardust Memories* is distorted and grotesque. Where Harold Cohen is resigned, Sandy Bates is despairing. All the elements which are used in *Stardust Memories* are well-known from Allen's other works, but the way in which they are used is new and completely devoid of hope and redemption.

The outer frame of the film is a weekend seminar, a Sandy Bates retrospect at the "Stardust Hotel." As in *Play It Again, Sam!* and *Annie Hall,* the plot structure is nonlinear, and the events are filtered through the imagination and memory of the protagonist. Because Sandy Bates's brain is more delirious than Alvy Singer's, the form of the movie becomes more complex, and the distinctions between delusive fantasy and reality much more diffuse than it was in the earlier works.

Sandy's philosophy of life is well-known from the previous Allen characters, but it has taken a disconsolate twist, which in part explains his psychological state and the distorted images that are presented to us on the screen. Like Alvy, Sandy is convinced that "the universe is gradually breaking down," but where Alvy and Isaac believed in potential redemption through morally commendable behavior, Sandy believes that everything is based on coincidence. Making "an effort" is thus not going to help you. What you need to make a relationship work, he says, is not the perfect mate and not compromise, but luck. It is coincidental that Sandy's friend, Nat Bernstein, and not Sandy himself, died of amytrophic sclerosis when he was thirty. It is coincidental that Sandy has achieved fame and fortune by having been born in a society "that puts a big value on jokes" and not as an Apache Indian: "those guys didn't need comedians at all." But the most incomprehensible coincidence is that, being a Jew born in the mid-1930s, he was born in Brooklyn and not in Nazi Germany: "I'd be a lampshade today, right?"

The relief which the earlier persona experienced through relationships is also denied Sandy. His only hope is in his past, in his "stardust memories" of his life with Dorrie. Sandy is presently involved with Isobel, who is a warm, mature, giving, and feminine character. All these traits are emphasized by her role as a mother. And, ironically enough, what Sandy likes about Isobel is also what he resents about her: her personality gives him what he most needs, but he is not so enthusiastic about her children. During this chaotic weekend, Isobel leaves her husband and comes to join Sandy at the "Stardust Hotel" with her children, with whom Sandy has obviously had no previous contact, nor indeed given any serious thought to. During Sandy's one scene with the infuriatingly noisy imps, he stares frantically out the window and dreams up a fantastic incident between himself and Dorrie in which she is giving him presents.[10]

Sandy's scenes with Isobel are ominously annoying. When he wants to talk seriously about their future, Isobel starts doing her facial exercises which make her look like she is "having a fit." When they are driving in Sandy's Rolls Royce on the way back from a chaotic visit to his sister's, his chauffeur gets arrested. And very significantly in the context of *Annie Hall* and *Manhattan*, Isobel, because of her children, is incapable of going to see *The Bicycle Thief* with him.

During the weekend seminar, Sandy meets Daisy to whom he feels attracted mainly because she reminds him of Dorrie. Unlike Isobel, she is free to go to the movies with him. Daisy is important in her function as a potential escape from Isobel, and in that most of Sandy's "stardust memories" are triggered off by something she does or says. Sandy is highly nostalgic about his past, and despite Dorrie's neuroses and hysteria (she is Isobel's absolute antithesis), their moments together seem much warmer and more comforting than any other scenes in the film. In one flashback, Sandy is chasing pigeons out of his apartment with a fire extinguisher because "they're rats with wings," while Dorrie is laughing, calling to mind the lobster scene in *Annie Hall*. In another, one of the loveliest scenes in any Allen movie, Sandy remembrs a Sunday with Dorrie. She is lying on the floor reading the Sunday paper. The sun is shining through the windows, Sandy is eating Häagen-Dazs ice cream. In the background we hear a record of Louis Armstrong singing *Stardust*, which song, with its melancholy premonition of separation, reminds us how valuable this moment is. And because we know how bleak Sandy's future looks, even their—chronologically—last scene together, where Sandy visits

Dorrie in a sanatorium after her breakdown, seems strangely reassuring despite the stark, uncanny background, the photography and editing and the tragic circumstances.

Finally the *shlemiel*'s comic release, which was Sandy's bread-and-butter in the past, is no longer possible for him. He does not want to make funny movies anymore because "I look around the world, and all I see is human suffering." Likewise, *Stardust Memories* is Allen's only movie to date which does not have any character with any of the *shlemiel*'s characteristics. One of the central dramatic tensions in the film is created when all through the weekend Sandy is constantly accosted by critics, fans, studio executives, and even, in one of the surreal scenes, by extraterrestrials, all of whom seem to agree that he has betrayed them, and that his earlier, funny movies were better than those he is making now. There is in this motif obvious parallels to the unreasonably negative critique of Allen's own first serious movie, *Interiors*. One critic that comes to mind is James Monaco, who speaks of "personal betrayal," of how "we have depended on Allen," how "Woody has gone over to the enemy," and how his serious films are "heartbreakingly disappointing."[11] No wonder Woody Allen found it necessary to deflate these *kvetching* critics.

We are constantly reminded of elements in Allen's earlier movies that are morbidly distorted here. Where Allan Felix had his walls covered with posters of old Humphrey Bogart movies, Sandy Bates has images of *his* obsessions—death and decay—sickeningly displayed on his. Where Allan Felix was dwarfed by the larger-than-life-size poster of *Across the Pacific* over his bed, Sandy's feeling of despair is visualized when *he,* in one of the first scenes of *Stardust Memories,* is dwarfed by a larger-than-life-size photo of the famous incident of the Saigon chief of police executing a Viet-Cong suspect for Eddie Adams's cameras. Where the *shlemiel* used his humor to survive the horrors of the world, Sandy Bates gives up comedy and self-destructively surrounds himself with images of horrors so as to constantly remind himself of the mouldering universe.

Similarly Sandy's fans call to mind the scene in *Annie Hall* in which two men in leather jackets, "the cast of *The Godfather*," start making a scene in front of the Beekman theater because they want Alvy's autograph. Whereas they—as seen through Alvy's eyes—are stupid and annoying, the fans in *Stardust Memories*—as seen through Sandy's—are ugly, malicious, pompous intruders who firmly believe that he can solve their petty problems. They are, as

Chaplin's disillusioned Calvero said—after Chaplin had "betrayed" *his* audience with the hostile *Monsieur Verdoux*—"a monster without a head."

Toward the end, the movie gets increasingly surreal, the division between fantasy and reality becomes nonexistent, and Sandy is clearly approaching a nervous breakdown. Yet, after a scene of death and rebirth—in which Sandy hallucinates that he is assassinated by a fan and faints—we get the only indication of hope in the film. The reborn Sandy tells the Sunday afternoon story about Dorrie and then gives her up. He finally makes up his mind that he wants to keep Isobel, who has decided to leave him, and he follows her onto a train, persuades her to stay, and tells her of the optimistic ending of his new film.

This hopefulness, however, is immediately and astonishingly undercut. In the very first scene of *Stardust Memories,* we see Sandy on a train full of distorted and grotesque looking people. The only sound we hear is that of a ticking clock, while Sandy is trying mutely to explain to the conductor that there has been a mistake and that he should be on another train that runs parallel to theirs, full of young, beautiful people. The ultimate destination of the two trains, however, proves to be identical: a junkyard full of screaming sea gulls. This pessimistic, nightmarish view of life turns out not to be the opening of the plot but rather the opening of Sandy's new movie, as we realize when the next shot shows the tail end of a piece of film in a projector and five upset executives who did not like it.

At the end of *Stardust Memories,* Sandy tells Isobel that his despair is over and that he has decided that the end of his new film should be more optimistic:

> "We're on a train and . . . I have no idea where it's headin' . . . could be the same junkyard. But it's not as terrible as I originally thought it was because you know, we like each other, and—and . . . uh, you know, we have some laughs, and there's a lot of closeness, and the whole thing is a lot easier to take."

Just as we relax and feel safe that once again personal relationships will eventually be able to ease the pain of the persona, Allen plays exactly the same trick on us a second time. The film cuts to an audience getting up from their seats and leaving a theater. We recognize the audience as the actors who were in the film, and they are now discussing their own and each other's roles and performances. Our attempts to figure out what was fantasy, what was reality, and what were clips of Sandy's old films have been completely futile. It was all film.

The character called Sandy Bates is removed even further from us when we realize that he was not the central character of the film, but the central character of the film within the film. And the characters called Dorrie, Daisy, and Isobel do not exist but are played by actors, who are in turn played by other actors, namely Charlotte Rampling, Jessica Harper, and Marie-Christine Barrault. At one point in the film we encounter the typical male friend of the Allen persona. In this film, however, he is not only played by Tony Roberts but indeed called Tony Roberts. Like at the end of *Annie Hall*, Woody Allen has managed to trick us into accepting the narrative basis of his film as reality. In the earlier film, we saw Alvy staging a play and comparing it (art) to his life (reality), thus confirming our belief. At the end of *Stardust Memories*, we are made brutally aware of the fallacy of our assumption.

One further result of this ending is a curious self-consciousness on the part of the audience of *Stardust Memories* when they get up and leave the theater after having just watched another audience do the same thing, an audience who had watched what we thought we were watching. Knowing how much the Allen persona—and presumably Allen himself—hates pontificating bores, this almost seems like a conscious act on Allen's part to make sure that nobody makes smart comments about his film on their way out of the theater. If they do, they are bound to sound like the man in the *Annie Hall* movie line, or like two of the *Stardust Memories* actors on their way out of the theater:

> *Charlotte:* What did you think the significance of the Rolls Royce was?
> *Lawyer:* I think that's . . . uh, uh, represents his car.

When a lot of people felt at the time of its release that *Stardust Memories* makes a fool of its audience, they were right. Not, as is generally felt, because its contemptuous depiction of Sandy's fans might indicate Woody Allen's vehement dislike of his, but rather because of this ending. Our credulity has been debunked and the joke, without doubt, is on us for having accepted a film as reality. One can almost see Allen, like Allan Felix sniggering to Bogart, "They bought it!" *Stardust Memories* not only portrays an Allen persona suffering from the delusive "side effects" of his obsessions for whom the only hope lies in the past, it ultimately dissuades its audience from trusting the movie itself. This endorsement to give up "faith in people" is Allen's ultimate expulsion of the *shlemiel* figure. For the first time we do not find a trace of him in any of the characters. We saw how the Allen persona, after an abiding development, shed his *shlemiel* status. Now after the *shlemiel* figure has been presented to us in a number of highly imaginative guises, he disappears from Allen's work altogether . . at least for a little while.

In 1981, after an interval of more than a decade, Allen opened a full-length play on Broadway. *The Floating Lightbulb* is his first attempt at serious drama, and it is so different from *Don't Drink the Water!* and *Play It Again, Sam!* that it is hard to believe that it was written by the same person. Like *Interiors,* this new play is a family drama, but unlike *Interiors,* it deals not with a well-to-do contemporary gentile family, but with a lower-class Jewish one in the 1950s. Allen's first noncomic drama, like his first noncomic film, is highly derivative, and its characters, as well as its dramatic tensions, are so well-known that ultimately they become facile and uninteresting.

As in *Interiors,* the mother, Enid, is the motivating force. Her "stardust" dreams of the past, of wasted possibilities, and of old beaux call to mind several of Tennessee Williams's female characters, as does her abortive romance with the theatrical manager, Jerry Wexler. Similarly, the father, Max, who feels that he never used his potential and tries to make up his mind whether to stay with his family or leave with his much younger mistress, resembles Arthur Miller's Willy Loman. Like Willy, Max repeatedly tries to improve his disastrous relationship with his two sons. Finally, more than anything else, the setting and the mood of the play call to mind Clifford Odets.

The most original element in the play is the young boy, Paul, who is a variation over Allen's *shlemiel.* Paul is so shy and introverted that he stays in his room all day to practice his magic tricks—a habit that Allen himself had as a child. His favorite trick is the "floating lightbulb." Enid, with her crude and pushy manners and her lust for the American dream, is the absolute antithesis to magic. She breaks Paul's illusion, nearly destroying him in the process, when she invites the unsuccessful theatrical manager Jerry Wexler to come and see Paul's "act."

Another noteworthy fact in terms of Allen's previous work is that *The Floating Lightbulb* deals not with more or less stable relationships between unmarried or divorced characters, but with an age-old marriage between people of Allen's parents' generation. They are the "Montagues and Capulets" that Cohen talks about in "Retribution." In his next film, for the first time Woody Allen plays a character who is married to the same woman at the beginning and at the end of the movie.

After making his most negative, hostile, and morbid film, Woody Allen proceeded to create what in many ways is the friendliest and most optimistic work of his entire career. In fact, the Ingmar Bergman film in which *A Midsummer Night's Sex Comedy* has its roots is the playful and droll *Smiles of a Summer Night*. *A Midsummer Night's Sex Comedy* is set not in contemporary New York but in a pastoral turn-of-the-century country house and its surrounding forests. In the film, however, the unfamiliar nonurban setting does not represent a threat the way it did in Allen's early works, but helps to transform the well-known conflicts and complexities of the Allen persona and finally solve them.

The characters and their problems are completely Allenesque: Adrian and Andrew, who own the country house, have been married for several years and their sex-life is practically nonexistent. Their guests for the weekend are Leopold, the pontificating realist, who is about to be married to the much younger Ariel, who turns out to be an old flame of Andrew's; Maxwell, who is the typical promiscuous male friend of the Allen persona and Maxwell's girlfriend—for the weekend—is Dulcy, who is a true child of nature and "radiates a certain raw energy." The comic situation of the film evolves around these three fickle New York couples and their infatuation with each others' partners.

Like several of the earlier Allen characters, Andrew believes in magic. Unlike them, however, he does not do magic tricks but is an inventor. He is convinced that there is an "unseen world"—things in life and the universe that we cannot see. He has thus invented a "spirit ball" by means of which, so he claims, these can be discovered. For Leopold, the realist academic, "nothing is real but experience," and he has no patience with Andrew's theories: "Apart from this world there are no realities." Maxwell, who is a doctor, calls Leopold a "pompous ass" and is more open to Andrew's ideas of a spirit world because "that's where all his patients end up." He still claims, however, that he only believes in "science and sex."

By the end of the film, both Leopold and Maxwell are converted. Leopold, while making love with Dulcy, has a heart attack and dies. As Andrew's spirit box suddenly turns on, the five other characters watch his spirit fly away, while the deceased Leopold has to admit that there *is* a "different dimension," "these woods *are* enchanted." Ariel, after finally making love with Andrew, discovers that she loves neither him nor Leopold but Maxwell, who reciprocates her feelings because, as he says: "We're two of a kind: flirts." Maxwell realizes that marriage does not have to be the "death of hope," but can indeed be its fulfillment. Andrew discovers that sleeping with his old love Ariel was not "what I thought it would be. . . . I don't think the old magic is there anymore." Adrian, in turn, admits that the reason why she could not sleep with Andrew is that she feels guilty for having slept with Maxwell a year ago, but now that "a curse has been lifted" she can make love with him again. Shortly afterward when the two of them come out of the barn, Andrew mutters that it was "a deeply religious experience on that table."

A Midsummer Night's Sex Comedy is an extremely enjoyable film. Apart from the charming plot, it has a number of beautifully photographed nature scenes which, combined with Felix Mendelsohn's enchanting music from *A Midsummer Night's Dream,* are completely breathtaking, and very unusual in the context of Allen's films. In addition, however, it is interesting in that it picks up and solves most of the obsessions of Woody Allen's earlier works.

The preoccupation with magic/dream versus reality, and the cruel universe have merged, so that magic in this film does not mean magic tricks but the "unseen world," the hidden things in the universe, which are as much a part of reality as any objective "truth." Furthermore, as opposed to Allen's other works, magic actually works in this movie. The magic box does not break down like the one in "The Kugelmass Episode." Magic is not a way of escaping reality, the way it was in *Don't Drink the Water!* and *The Floating Lightbulb,* but a way of seeing it more clearly. Thus Andrew is not blinded by his magic the way Allan Felix was by the magic of Hollywood, but is actually made more perceptive by it. At the end of *Play It Again, Sam!,* Dick and Linda went to Cleveland on a plane, while Allan, who had come *down* to reality, stayed on the ground. In *Bananas,* Fielding Mellish's degrading was visualized when, having just envisaged an elaborate seduction of Nancy, he fell into a manhole. Finally, in *A Midsummer Night's Sex Comedy,* the Allen persona literally manages to transcend reality by means of the winged bicycle he has invented.

Not only does magic work in *A Midsummer Night's Sex Comedy,* love does too. In the early films, the Allen persona often ended up *getting* the girl, and in the middle ones he was obsessed with having *lost* her. In this film, Andrew and Adrian stay together in spite of their problems and ultimately manage to solve them. In an interview in connection with the release of *A Midsummer Night's Sex Comedy,* Woody Allen said: "I think good sex depends on being in love with a person. I mean good erotic, dirty sex—the kind you grow up wanting to have all your life—comes from being in love with a person, having real feelings."[12] In this film, sex is indeed not preferable to love or the other way around, they are closely interconnected. Thus Andrew and Adrian's marriage cannot work without sex, and reciprocally, when Andrew sleeps with Ariel, he realizes that sex without love is not so "magical" either. His assertion at the beginning of the film, when he is frustrated because of his wife's reluctance to sleep with him, that you can separate the two—"Sex alleviates tension: love causes it"—is finally proven wrong by himself. Rather than marriage being, as Maxwell claims at the beginning of the film, "the death of hope," it is seen, in Oscar Wilde's words, as "hope's triumph over experience."

So in Woody's Allen's tenth film, hope does triumph once again, and all the threads are gathered up and tied together in the most reassuring manner. Magic works and helps you see reality, if only you have the faith. Love is not an abortive and hopeless experience about which the only sensible thing one can say is "Oy Vey!" but a valuable and fruitful possibility for real fulfillment in life if you are willing to make the effort. The universe and death are no longer cruel and inhumane but magical and enchanted. And the Allen persona, finally, is no longer the neurotic and suspicious misanthrope who is inhibited by his obsession with morality, but a slightly confused person for whom happiness is a very real and desirable possibility. Thus with *A Midsummer Night's Sex Comedy,* the Allen persona resumes the *shlemiel*-role that he shed several years earlier. He is now a fully developed mature *shlemiel* who believes in fantasy *and* reality, uses his mind *and* his body, his heart *and* his brain. He believes in a benevolent universe and the possibility of lasting relationships, and has at least a little faith in people.

One can only guess whether this new optimism in Woody Allen had anything to do with Mia Farrow's entering and replenishing his life and works.

6

Isn't It Romantic? (1983–1986)

We are haunted not by reality, but by those images we have put
in the place of reality.[1]

—Daniel Boorstin

Having worked his way toward a solution of the "contemporary
conflicts" of his narcissist persona, Woody Allen moved on to fresh
territory in his next three films: *Zelig, Broadway Danny Rose,* and
The Purple Rose of Cairo. All three, like *A Midsummer Night's Sex
Comedy,* are set in the "stardust" past, and all three are miniatures
basically evolving around one conflict or problem.

In his account of the immigration of the East European Jews
around the turn of the century, *World of Our Fathers,* Irving Howe
writes, refering to all Jews living in the diaspora:

> The need to adjust to conditions of life in a strange country first
> became a problem for other groups only in America; but for Jews it
> was a problem they had had to face for many centuries. Others came
> to their new country with one culture; the Jews came with two, and
> frequently more than two, cultures. One culture they carried deep
> *within* themselves, within their spiritual and psychic being. The other
> they bore *upon* themselves, like an outer garment.[2]

The title character of Woody Allen's next film *Zelig* is in a sense the
embodiment of this theory.

In a collage of vintage newsreels, new footage, old records, and
interviews with well-known intellectuals, all held together by a
voice-over narrator, Allen returns to the mock-documentary style
of *Take the Money and Run!,* to tell the strange story of Leonard
Zelig, one of the great psychological phemonena of the early
decades of the twentieth century. Because he had an extremely
traumatic childhood, the adult Zelig is so insecure and afraid of
standing out, that he develops a peculiar trait. Whenever he is in

the same room with someone who has a stronger personality than himself—i.e., virtually anyone—he begins, emotionally *and* physically, to resemble that person. Thus a 1928 entry—the first recorded notice taken of Leonard Zelig—is found in F. Scott Fitzgerald's diary:

> [He] seemed clearly to be an aristocrat and extolled the very rich as he chatted with socialites. He spoke adoringly of Coolidge and the Republican Party, all in an upperclass Boston accent. An hour later, I was stunned to see the same man speaking with the kitchen help. Now he claimed to be a democrat, and his accent seemed to be coarse as if he were one of the crowd.

The following year, a waiter in a Chicago speakeasy sees Zelig, first as a tough-looking white mobster, then, only a few minutes later, as a black trumpet player in the band. A couple of months after that incident, a clerk named Leonard Zelig disappears. The authorities find him in an opium den, and all the way to Manhattan Hospital "he rants in what sounds like authentic Chinese."

After several experiments, the doctors realize that Zelig's various physiognomical shapes are not disguises. He actually metamorphoses into a Frenchman, a Scot, a Chinese, and—when psychiatrist Eudora Fletcher interviews him—Sigmund Freud. They cannot agree on a diagnosis, though. One doctor is convinced that the "disease" is glandular, another that it is neurological, a third claims that it must be "something he picked up from eating Mexican food."

Dr. Fletcher is certain that the origin of Zelig's malady is psychological. She puts him under hypnosis and finds that ever since childhood he has been bullied by others. Whenever the anti-Semitic toughs in his neighborhood beat him up, his parents took their side. So at an early age Zelig decided that "it's safe to be like the others," and when the intelligent children at school were discussing *Moby Dick,* Leonard Zelig—for the first time trying to blend in—pretended that he too had read it.

When the newspapers start publishing stories of the case that Dr. Fletcher has named "the human chameleon," Zelig's half-sister Ruth and her fiancé, an ex-carnival promoter, remove him from the hospital and put him on exhibition: "See Leonard Zelig turn into you," their advertising sign reads. On a tour to Spain, Ruth falls in love with a mediocre bullfighter, and her fiancé kills the two of them and commits suicide. Zelig disappears, and Dr. Fletcher is distressed.

In 1929, Zelig is discovered on the balcony in Rome with Pope

Pius XI. He is brought back to New York and finally turned over to Eudora Fletcher who brings him to her country home. After months of analysis and hypnosis Zelig is cured, and becomes the toast of the town. Quite unexpectedly disaster strikes again. In his various guises Zelig turns out to have committed several morally reprehensible crimes, and he is sued for everything from polygamy and fraud to taking out an appendix. The fickle public turns against him. Zelig, who was to be married to Dr. Fletcher, instead suffers a relapse, turns into a Greek, and disappears.

Dr. Fletcher never stops searching for him and finally finds him at a giant Nazi rally in Munich. The two of them try to escape from the Nazis, but Eudora Fletcher panics. Because she is a pilot, however, Zelig turns into one, and they manage to get away, at the same time breaking the record for "flying across the Atlantic nonstop upside-down."

Fletcher and Zelig get married, gradually all Zelig's symptoms disappear, and they live happily ever after. On his deathbed, Zelig's only regret is that he still has not finished reading *Moby Dick*.

In many ways, *Zelig* marks a turning point in Allen's career. From a concern with the culture of narcissism, he has moved on to a concern with the culture of celebrity, which to some extent is characteristic of his next two films as well. In his book, *The Image*, Daniel Boorstin states that the mass produced celebrity of the twentieth century is someone who is "well-known for his well-knownness."[3] Boorstin outlines the differences between today's celebrity and yesterday's hero thus:

> [In the past] a man's name was not apt to become a household word unless he exemplified greatness in some way or other. He might be a Napoleon, great in power, a J. P. Morgan, great in wealth, a St. Francis, great in virtue, or a Bluebeard, great in evil. . . . Within the last century, and especially since about 1900, we seem to have discovered the processes by which fame is manufactured. Now, . . . a man's name can become a household word overnight. The Graphic Revolution suddenly gave us, among other things, the means of fabricating well-knownness. . . . The household names, the famous men, who populate our consciousness are with few exceptions not heroes at all, but an artificial new product. . . . We can fabricate fame, we can at will (though usually at considerable expense) make a man or woman well known; but we cannot make him great.[4]

In the true spirit of P. T. Barnum—one of the people discussed in Boorstin's book—Zelig's sister and her fiancé discover the mar-

ketability of "the human chameleon." They make him an over-
night celebrity, and a nationwide Zelig craze begins. Zelig dolls,
pens, watches, and earmuffs are sold all over the country. A
chameleon dance is invented, and several popular records are
inspired by the phenomenon: "Leonard, the Lizzard," "Reptile
Eyes," "You May Be Six People, but I Love You." According to one
witness, Cole Porter even wrote a line in his famous song: "You're
the top, you are Leonard Zelig, . . . but then he could not find
anything to rhyme with Zelig."

Boorstin discusses the case of Charles Lindbergh, a hero who
was degraded to the status of celebrity, whose feat, a real historical
event, was turned into a pseudo-event by the press. Finally the
kidnapping of his son was, Boorstin says, "as spectacular as
Lindbergh's translantic flight."[5]

In his recent book, *Intimate Strangers,* Richard Schickel sheds
light on new and fascinating aspects of the culture of celebrity. His
most illuminating argument concerns "the psychopathic loner"—
one example of which would be John Hinckley, Jr.—who so
longed to get attention (in this case Jodie Foster's) that he was
prepared to kill for it. Schickel incomprehendingly speculates
about

> the wildly parodistic version of celebrity treatment that is accorded the
> criminal who has assaulted a well-known person. He gets a police
> escort and a motorcade whenever he emerges in public. He gets to
> make his well-guarded passages through crowds of the curious. He
> gets to feel the flashing lights of the photographers turned on him,
> hear the shouted questions of the reporters. For the first time in his
> hitherto anonymous life people will be curious about his history, his
> thoughts. In due course, his ravings may find their way into print. Or
> he will have his story told by a famous novelist.[6]

An even more recent example of this type of celebrity is, of
course, Bernhard Goetz whose shooting of four teenagers on a
New York subway train in December of 1984 bore an uncanny
resemblance to a scene in the Charles Bronson film *Death Wish.*
Ironically, the fact that Goetz was heralded as a public hero for
doing so, echoes the ending of Martin Scorsese's masterpiece *Taxi
Driver.* It would seem that John Hinckley was not the only one who
was incapable of grasping the point of Scorsese's film.

Leonard Zelig is as much of a celebrity as the examples that
Boorstin and Schickel mention. In fact, according to Susan Sontag, one of several intellectuals who are interviewed throughout
the film, "he was *the* phenomenon of the 20s. We think at that

time, he was as well-known as Lindberg." Saul Bellow later assures us that it is "ironic to see how quickly he has faded from memory, considering what an astounding impact he made." But contrary to Charles Lindbergh, John Hinckley, and Scorsese's Travis Bickle, Leonard Zelig is reluctant and extremely unhappy about his fame. His only wish is to blend in, to go unnoticed.

Like the Jewish immigrants that Irving Howe discusses, Leonard Zelig has one identity which he carries "deep within [himself], within [his] spiritual and psychic being," namely his own, and several others that he can put on whenever he needs them. In effect he is an exaggerated version of the assimilating Jew who tries to fit into whatever culture he happens to be living in. Howe—who is another of the "witnesses" in the film—describes Zelig's predicament thus: "When I think about it, it seems to me that his story reflected a lot of the Jewish experience in America, the great urge to push in and to find one's place, and then assimilate into the culture. I mean, he wanted to assimilate like crazy."

After his recovery, Zelig is asked to give speeches all over the country. The public now want to know his opinions (the same way they wanted Lindbergh's) on politics, art, life, and love. Boorstin says about Lindbergh: "His celebrity status unfortunately had persuaded him to become a public spokesman. When Lindbergh gave in to these temptations, he offended. . . . His pronouncements were dull, petulant, and vicious. He required a reputation as a pro-Nazi and a crude racist; he accepted a decoration from Hitler."[7] On the basis of *his* experience, Zelig gives this advice: "You have to be your own person and make your own moral choices, even when they do require real courage. . . . You have to be your own man and speak up and say what's on your mind. Maybe they're not free to do so in other countries, but that's the American way."

Like the other manifestations of the Allen persona before him, Leonard Zelig has realized the importance of taking a moral stand of one's own. No matter how dull or unimportant one's life seems, trying to escape it by being somebody else is not going to work. No matter how desperately Leonard Zelig would have liked to be assimilated, like Heywood Allen in the "Deep South routine" he could never run away from his own ethnicity. Before his recovery, he wanted only to be like everybody else, "to be liked" at any cost. Now he has realized that what really matters is not "the approbation of many, but the love of one woman." As in the early Allen films, the best solution to the problems of modern man is personal relationships.

The story of Leonard Zelig is filled with paradoxes, though. When he wanted only to blend in and go unseen by his enemies, Zelig ended up being constantly watched by the entire country. His fame was, in fact, based on his desire to fit in, to go unnoticed. On the other hand, he manages to escape the Nazis on an aeroplane *because of* his ability to transform himself. Thus, as Saul Bellow says, "his sickness was also at the root of his salvation." Finally, when he recovers, he is more assimilated than ever. Where most of his transformations were ethnic, he now sounds as true-blue American as Robert Redford in a Sydney Pollack film.

Furthermore the views that Zelig now has the courage to express are distinctly "lowbrow." At one point we hear fragments of his sessions with Doctor Fletcher, played over a series of still photos of the two of them relaxing together:

> I love baseball. You know, it doesn't have to mean anything, it's just very beautiful to watch.—I'm a democrat. I always was a democrat.—Is it okay if I don't agree with you about that recording? You know, Brahms is just always too melodramatic for me.—No, I don't agree. I think this guy Mussolini is a loser. . . . Are we ever going to make love?

Typically Allen intermingles discussions of sports and sex with speculations over politics and classical music.

In *Zelig,* as in Allen's earlier works, we see an enormous ambivalence toward cultural and intellectual issues. On the one hand a number of renowned intellectuals are asked to give their interpretation of the phenomenon "Leonard Zelig;" on the other their statements are treated in a tongue-in-cheek fashion, even by themselves.[8] Conversely we are definitely expected to respect Leonard Zelig's views. They may be rather proletarian, but at least they are his own. A very plausible reason, in fact, why Zelig never manages to read *Moby Dick,* even though he regrets it on his deathbed, may simply be that he prefers baseball.

As in E. L. Doctorow's best-selling novel *Ragtime*—which leaves off almost exactly where *Zelig* begins—the truly American culture is not the highbrow culture of Melville and Brahms, but precisely the popular, lowbrow culture of baseball. As one critic says:

> Whereas in Europe high and popular culture are strictly segregated and the influences are legitimized from the top down, in America the

two cultures are intertwined and the distinctively American impulses move from the bottom up. Ragtime and motion pictures, vaudeville and baseball were all nourished by contributors from the lowly group of immigrants and blacks.[9]

In its view of history as in its view of culture, Woody Allen's film resembles E. L. Doctorow's book.[10] All through Allen's career we have seen a consistent fascination with the elusive lines between fantasy and reality. Allan Felix had trouble distinguishing between the two, as did Alvy Singer with his "hyperactive imagination." Only in *A Midsummer Night's Sex Comedy* were the two reconciled. Now Allen plays another trick on us and promiscuously mixes fact and fiction. Not only does he, as in *Take the Money and Run!*, present a fictitious story to us, claiming that it is factual, he also lets invented characters mingle freely with historical characters. Zelig associates, as we have seen, with the famous and the infamous, Scott Fitzgerald, the pope, and Adolf Hitler. The only clue the police find in Zelig's apartment when he disappears is a photo of him with Eugene O'Neill.

In *Intimate Strangers* Richard Schickel describes how the typical piece of twentieth-century journalism "often at the expense of the traditional standards of the craft . . . employ[s] the techniques of fiction to enliven allegedly factual material and to give it a knowing tone."[11] What Allen and Doctorow do is exactly the opposite: they insert historical personages and events into their fictional frame and thereby imaginatively rewrite an era in American history, and in the process they reveal significant psychological, if not historical, truths about that era. Where Boorstin seemed confident that in the past "a man's name was not apt to become a household word unless he exemplified greatness,"[12] Allen and Doctorow alike have us convinced that history, past as well as contemporary, is based primarily on coincidence.

The historical past that is presented to us in *Zelig*, moreover, is, as Andrew Sarris said, a highly "stylized past masquerading as reality."[13] By employing a collage technique similar to that used by Orson Welles in *Citizen Kane*, Allen manages to transfer the period of the 1920s and 1930s to a plane which is parodistically mythical rather than literal. By mixing well-known authentic newsreels with invented ones, famous popular songs with adapted ones, and so forth, Allen not only blurs the distinctions between fact and fiction, but revealingly points out the uncanny extent to which our conception of American history is fashioned by stereotypical media phenomena. He illustrates how, as Daniel Boorstin said, we "are haunted not by reality, but by those images we have put in the place of reality."[14]

As Allen explores new territory relating to his old obsession regarding fact versus fiction or dream versus reality in *Zelig,* so in his next film he has returned to yet another of his earlier concerns, namely the question of personal integrity and having a little faith in people. *Broadway Danny Rose* is a sort of Sholom-Aleichem-meets-Damon-Runyon-tale. The resemblance to Runyon's Broadway stories and the movies based on them (such as *Guys and Dolls* and *Angels over Broadway*) is obvious, and several of the characters in the film call to mind the familiar Runyon types. But in his impractical optimism the title character, Danny Rose, is more reminiscent of the great *luftmenshen* in Yiddish literature, such as Aleichem's Menachem Mendel.

The film opens at the Carnegie Delicatessen. Several middle-aged comics, among them Corbett Monica, Jack Rollins, Sandy Baron, Will Jordan, and Morty Gunty, sit around telling retrospective stories about themselves and their show business colleagues. Some of the stories deal with one Danny Rose. Danny is an insignificant way-off-Broadway personal manager who represents, among others, a one-legged tap dancer, a one-armed juggler, and a blind xylophonist. Danny is completely devoted to each and every one of his clients, but in the rare cases when one of them becomes famous, they always leave him.

Sandy Baron tells the central story of the film which concerns Danny Rose's one-time favorite client, Lou Canova, a moderately talented, overweight, middle-aged crooner with a drinking problem, a swelling ego, and a troubled love life. When a nostalgia craze sets in, Lou suddenly gets a lot of attention. Danny persuades Milton Berle, who needs someone to open his show at *Caesar's Palace,* to come and see Lou's act at the Waldorf. In preparation for this, Danny devotes all his time to Lou and his show, much to the consternation of his other clients. Lou seems confident of his own talent and success, and instead worries over how to bring his mistress, Tina Vitale, without his wife finding out. He asks Danny to bring her to the concert, pretending she is *his* date.

The big day arrives, and Danny reluctantly goes to New Jersey to pick up Tina. Now his troubles really begin. Tina turns out to be a brassy blond virago, who is also the widow of a mafioso. She has heard rumors that Lou has been seen with a "cheap blonde" (which is not unlikely since he is married to one) and refuses to come. With Danny following her, Tina goes to see Angelina, a fortune-teller, who advises her to solve the problems in her family. Danny follows Tina and finds that her family is having a party which looks like a black-and-white Felliniish version of the opening scene of *The Godfather*. Tina's old lover, whom she left for Lou, will not forgive her. Because Lou has been sending Tina a white rose every day, the family concludes that Danny Rose, whom they now call "Danny White Roses" is the suitor and must be killed.

The two brothers of the betrayed lover chase Danny and Tina all over New Jersey and Manhattan and finally take them to a huge warehouse. Danny hysterically assures the two mafiosi that he is not the man they are after. When they demand to know who Tina's real lover is, Danny, not wanting to betray his star, gives them the name of his friend, Barney Dunn, the stuttering ventriloquist, who has just gone on a cruise to the Bahamas for several weeks.

Danny and Tina are tied up but manage to escape, and they rush over to the Waldorf where they find Lou dead drunk. Danny miraculously gets him on his feet, and the concert is a smash hit. Afterward Lou tells Danny that Tina has persuaded him to get a new and better manager. Danny, who is really beginning to like Tina, feels betrayed and goes off by himself to get a cup of coffee and think things over. The waiter at the deli tells him that Barney Dunn's cruise was cancelled and that Barney is now in the hospital because he has been assaulted and beaten up. Danny is devastated and rushes over to the Roosevelt Hospital and offers to pay Barney's hospital bill.

Lou leaves his wife and moves in with Tina. He is extremely preoccupied with his own success, but Tina is feeling guilty toward Danny and is getting moodier by the hour. After a while they split up. Tina moves in with a ham-actor, but her melancholia will not go away. Finally, on Thanksgiving, she decides to go and ask Danny's forgiveness. When she gets to his apartment, Danny is in the middle of a frozen turkey dinner with his friends and clients. Danny is reserved and will not invite the unhappy and repentant Tina in, so she leaves. Danny immediately regrets his coldness and starts running after her. He catches up with her in front of the Carnegie Deli. Sandy Baron, in a voice-over, concludes that "only six months ago they gave him the single greatest honor you can get in the Broadway area"; the Carnegie Delicatessen named a sandwich after him—the *Danny Rose Special*—a bagel with cream cheese and marinara sauce. After that, the story tellers agree that it is time to go home.

Broadway Danny Rose has a number of concerns in common with

Allen's previous films. Not only is it set in New York, but the city, which is shot in black and white like in *Manhattan,* takes on a mythical quality. The Danny Rose stories are undefinedly retrospective. They are set in a timeless New York City. The streets and locations around Broadway seem as fabled as in the Damon Runyon stories, and Danny Rose himself, in the familiar tradition of Sky Masterson, Nicely-Nicely Johnson, and Harry the Horse, is the big city person incarnate, "a living legend," as Sandy Baron says at the very end of the film. Likewise, the Carnegie Deli is given a mythical status similar to that of Mindy's in Runyon's tales.

As in all Allen's works, there is another tradition at work behind the American comic tradition, namely, the Yiddish literary tradition. Possibly the most famous Yiddish fictional character of all times is Sholom Aleichem's Tevye the Dairyman, the central character of Aleichem's play *Tevye and His Daughters,* later filmed as *Fiddler on the Roof.* Tevye's philosophy of life is extremely simple:

> As we say on Yom Kippur, the Lord decides who will ride on horseback and who will crawl on foot. The main thing is—hope! A Jew must always hope, must never lose hope. And in the meantime, what if we waste away to a shadow? For that we are Jews—the Chosen People, the envy and admiration of the world.[15]

Like most of Allen's *shlemiel* characters before him, Danny Rose has the capacity for hope and faith in other people. Despite the fact that his clients always leave him as soon as he has made them famous, he retains his faith in them and the hope that someday things will change.

Also, like Alvy Singer and Ike Davis, Danny Rose is a dogmatic moralist who believes in personal responsibility and integrity. His idiosyncratic moral code is made up from Yiddish folklore wisdom, i.e. quotations from various family members. Thus, when Lou, the typically self-indulgent male friend of the Allen persona, insists that he cannot live without Tina, Danny starts pontificating in his characteristically gesticulating fashion and endlessly complicated sentences:

> I've always tried to teach you Lou, that sooner or later, you're gonna have to square yourself with the Big Guy. . . . You're gonna pay your dues someday, you know. You're a married man. My aunt Rose, take my aunt Rose, not a beautiful woman at all, she looks like something you'd buy in a live bait store, but why, she had wisdom and she used to say: "You can't ride two horses with one behind!" So you see what I'm saying?

His miraculous remedy against stage fright for his clients is a simple three-word sentence: "Star, Smile, Strong!"

Danny is astounded when Tina tells him of her life philosophy: "It's over quick, so have a good time. You see what you want, go for it. Don't pay any attention to anybody else and do it to the other guy first 'cause if you don't, he'll do it to you." "This is a philosophy of life," Danny incomprehendingly asks. "It sounds like the screenplay to *Murder Incorporated*." Like his late uncle Sidney, Danny believes that what really counts in life is "acceptance, forgiveness, and love."

Broadway Danny Rose, like Allen's previous films, is concerned with the values of friendships and the betrayal that is often involved. At the center of the film we have Lou's and Tina's betrayal of Danny, and Danny's betrayal of Barney Dunn. Like a number of earlier characters, Danny rose is a firm believer in personal integrity, and, according to the familiar preoccupation in Allen's films with the repercussions of McCarthyism, Danny commits an unforgiveable sin when he cooperates and gives the two gangsters Barney Dunn's name.

In Tina we likewise find echoes of Allen's earlier films.[16] Her fortune-teller Angelina, is a tongue-in-cheek Catholic analogue to the Allen persona's psychoanalyst. There is constantly a long line of people in her parlour who want her to tell them how to run their lives. Tina's surname, Vitale, suggests that she has inherited some of the life-giving aspects of the *shlemiel* role. Admittedly, most of her family seems to be in the life-*taking* profession, and she certainly does not have the warm loving personality that Annie, Pearl, and Tracy did, but she *is* capable of bringing joy and laughter into Danny Rose's life.

Danny's own philosohy of life sounds as if it was taken right out of Alvy Singer's mouth: "It's important to have some laughs, no question about it, but you got to suffer a little too, because otherwise you miss the whole point of life." At the end of the film, Danny realizes that he does not, in fact, want the buoyant Tina to walk out of his life, and in a scene very reminiscent of the ending of *Manhattan*, he runs after her. Contrary to the earlier film, however, it looks as if Danny and Tina make up on the spot, and that there is a chance for them instantly.

In the early part of Allen's career, the endings of his films were rather awkward, as if he could not figure out how to stop them. Just think of *Bananas* and *Sleeper*. In the period from *Annie Hall* to *Stardust Memories,* they were characterized by an idiosyncratic, bittersweet quality, with the emphasis on bitter. The ending of

Broadway Danny Rose is typical of Allen's films in the period after *Stardust Memories*. They, too, have a slightly bittersweet tone, but now the emphasis is definitely on sweet. *A Midsummer Night's Sex Comedy* had a very pleasant happy ending with Andrew and Ariel making up, and Leonard Zelig's peculiar destiny likewise ended with a happy marriage. Like *Broadway Danny Rose,* all Allen's films made in the early 1980s have this sweet and extremely enjoyable quality, which seems very closely connected with Mia Farrow's characters. This tendency culminates in Allen's next film, *The Purple Rose of Cairo.*

In 1977, Woody Allen received an O'Henry Award for his short story "The Kugelmass Episode." Its subject matter was middle-aged Professor Sidney Kugelmass and his desire to have some romance in his life. Kugelmass goes to a magician, who, by means of a magic box, projects him into Gustave Flaubert's *Madame Bovary.*[17] To a certain extent, Woody Allen's thirteenth film, *The Purple Rose of Cairo,* is a visualization of the idea that formed the basis for "The Kugelmass Episode."

It is set in a drab town in New Jersey in 1935, i.e., during the Great Depression. Its central character, Cecilia, is a worn out little waitress, who is hopeless at her job because of her tendency to daydream. Her husband, Monk, is a lazy hulk of a man who cheats on her and beats her up. Her only escape from her dull life is the local movie theater, the Jewel, and she rarely misses a performance of the Hollywood romances shown there every night. One night, when she watches the film of the week, "The Purple Rose of Cairo," for the fourth time, its hero, Tom Baxter, a handsome young adventurer who has been searching in vain for the "legendary purple rose," addresses her. He wishes to talk to her, he says, and then he proceeds to step down from his black-and-white screen. The results are chaotic: Tom falls in love with Cecilia and refuses to go back to his film. The other characters of the film—or rather the film-within-the-film—cannot continue without him.

Tom turns out to be completely helpless in "the real world" because he is familiar only with the universe created for him by screenwriters Irving Sachs and R. H. Levine. Thus he talks in clichés, tries to pay for a fancy dinner with toy money, and when Cecilia's husband beats him up, neither his clothes nor his hair get the least bit rumpled. Gil Shepherd, the actor who plays Tom Baxter, comes out from Hollywood with the producers of the film to try and talk Tom into going back to the screen. Meanwhile the charming ham actor, Gil, falls in love with sweet and understanding Cecilia, who now has two admirers who look exactly alike but are extremely different. Cecilia is very confused, and in her desperation she says to Gil about Tom: "I just met a wonderful new man. He's fiction, but you can't have everything."

At the end of the film—as at the end of *Play It Again, Sam!*—everything is back to normal. Tom is back on his screen; Gil has gone back to Hollywood; and Cecilia has returned to her seat at the Jewel theater, which is now playing *Top Hat* with Fred Astaire and Ginger Rogers.

Certain aspects of *The Purple Rose of Cairo* are new and surprising in terms of Allen's works. Its setting is particularly fascinating. Who would have thought Woody Allen capable of describing a small suburban town with as much conviction and authenticity as he portrayed Manhattan in his previous films? The "contemporary conflicts" have given way to other more basic problems such as the possibilities of surviving an economic depression, physically as well as emotionally—themes that Allen touched on in *The Floating Lightbulb*. It has now been twelve years since Allen assured us that the "conflicts of the Depression, or having to make a living, or guys working in factories" had no relevance for a contemporary audience.[18] Apparently Allen has broadened his intellectual universe since then. Thus, this small town depression milieu is extremely moving, and, for Allen, very unusually filmed in what Pauline Kael calls "the deep *Godfather* browns."[19]

Despite a number of rather superficial surprises, *The Purple Rose of Cairo* is thematically extremely closely connected with Allen's earlier works. Like a number of these, from *Take the Money and Run* to *Zelig* and *Broadway Danny Rose*, it deals with topics such as fantasy versus reality, fact versus fiction, the influence of Hollywood on our lives, and having a little faith in people. We are presented with "layers" of reality. The film we are watching is called *The Purple Rose of Cairo,* but so is the film Cecilia is watching at the Jewel Theater. Tom Baxter is played by Gil Shepherd who, in turn, is played by Jeff Daniels. As in Allen's previous works, there is an implication that Tom Baxter's film is fiction whereas Cecilia's world is "real life." When Cecilia has to choose between the fictitious Tom Baxter and the "factual" Gil Shepherd, she apologizes to Tom: "No matter how tempted I am, I have to choose the real world." Too late she realizes that Gil Shepherd is no more part of the real world than Tom Baxter. He is as elusive as the fictitious Tom, and leaves her without saying goodbye. Finally, her only reality is her uncomfortable little seat at the Jewel Theater.

Furthermore, on the basis of *Play it Again, Sam!, Stardust Memories,* and *Zelig,* it is hardly surprising when Allen breaks the realistic conventions and lets Tom step down from the screen and into Cecilia's world. We have already seen that trying to transfer the ethics of Hollywood to "the real world" inevitably has disastrous consequences. Thus Tom's inability to function in Cecilia's world is predictable. Like the Bogart figure in *Play It Again, Sam!,* he is two-dimensional, pompous, and extremely limited. Ultimately his world is not as desirable as it may seem.

Indeed, just as the real hero of *Play It Again, Sam!* was not Humphrey Bogart, but Allan Felix, so the real hero of this film is neither the glamorous Tom Baxter nor the self-content Gil Shephard, but little, insecure Cecilia. She trusts the men in her life completely and is exploited by each one of them in turn. Like Annie Hall, Pearl, and Tracy, she has—with her infinite faith in people—taken over the life-giving characteristics of the *shlemiel* persona. Like Tom in the film-within-the-film she defies her destiny by refusing to give up her search for the kind of romantic love which is symbolized by the legendary purple rose of Cairo. But—according to Allen's morale—what matters is the fact that you keep searching; whether you reach your goal or not is less relevant. Likewise it is the *shlemiel's* and Cecilia's faith in people that really matters, not whether people live up to their expectations.

According to an article by Nick Rosen, "Hurricane Woody Hits Town," certain people apparently felt that Allen himself, during the filming of *The Purple Rose of Cairo,* did not live up to their faith in him. The film was to be shot on location in a small town named Piermont, about fifteen miles north of New York City. The shooting was scheduled to start at the beginning of November of 1983 and to end about ten to fourteen days later. According to Rosen, the first problems arose when not everybody would agree to let Allen use their house for the $200 fee that he offered. Some agreed when they were offered $300, others took $400, and a number of people managed to get $1,000 out of the deal. The result, according to one house owner, Len Sullivan, was that those "who had taken $200 were madder than hell."[20]

Later Allen demanded that the inhabitants of the town remove their storm windows for aesthetic reasons. No sooner had they done so when a fierce blizzard set in. The damages were immense, and the repair work took time. The shooting itself took not ten days but three and a half weeks. The month of December began, but because the shopping area was sealed off, the locals could not do their Christmas shopping. The stores suffered great losses, and some went bankrupt. In May 1984, seven months after the first members of the crew arrived, contractors, according to Rosen, were still working in Piermont trying to get things back to normal.

What finally makes *The Purple Rose of Cairo* worth all that trouble is primarily the Mia Farrow character. Although the roles that Farrow has played in Allen's films are all extremely different (and certainly miles away from the roles she used to play), one could argue that she has established a persona of her own in these films. In her review of *Zelig,* Pauline Kael used adjectives like luminous, unearthly, refined, finely chiselled, and beautiful to describe Mia Farrow. Like a chameleon, Farrow has, as Kael says, become "as faded and indistinct as [Allen] is."[21] It almost seems as if some sort of metamorphosis has taken place, and not only with Leonard Zelig. Mia Farrow has started gesticulating and has adopted some of Allen's facial expressions, so that in certain scenes she too resembles a fluttering insect, the way Heywood Allen did in the early routines, and the way Allen himself does in *Broadway Danny Rose.* Conversely, Allen's films have taken on a much sweeter, less neurotic quality. In fact they, like Farrow, are luminous, unearthly, refined, finely chiselled, and beautiful. They no longer have the frantic quality that the preceding films did, and neither does the Woody Allen character. Mia Farrow's influence seems to have changed him as well.

In Allen's very early films, we saw a basic conflict between the mind and the body. One could argue that the objective correlative of that conflict was the relationship between the Woody Allen character and the Louise Lasser character: Allen representing the fragile body, and Lasser representing the fickle brain. In the later films, the conflict between the mind and the body was replaced by a conflict between the heart and the brain. As we have already seen, the relationship between the Allen persona and the Diane Keaton characters to a great extent reflected that conflict.

In the three miniatures that Allen made after having resolved all his major concerns in *A Midsummer Night's Sex Comedy,* however, there is no basic conflict. This is partly due to the fact that the Mia Farrow persona does not, as Pauline Kael says, challenge the Allen persona as Diane Keaton did in her films with him. The central elements in these charming "essays" seem to form a synthesis, and all the Allen persona's anhedonic tendencies and tensions seem miraculously to have vanished. Isn't that romantic?

7

I've Heard That Song Before (1987–1989)

I closed the book and felt this strange mixture of wistfulness
and hope. And I wondered if a memory is something you have
or something you've lost. For the first time in a long time I felt
at peace.[1]

—Woody Allen, *Another Woman*

Shortly after Woody Allen turned forty, he wrote, directed, and
starred in a film that was intelligent, bittersweetly romantic, and
breathtakingly superior to anything he had ever done before,
namely *Annie Hall*. On February 7, 1986, just a few months after
his fiftieth birthday, Allen's fourteenth film, *Hannah and Her Sisters*, was released—a film which compares to *Annie Hall* in that it is
one of the most moving, and most skillfully directed, and in that it
completely overshadows the works that preceded it. Allen's
movies of the early 1980s were small, relatively uncomplicated,
and very enjoyable vignettes that, for all their aesthetic beauty and
despite—or perhaps actually because of—their lack of a basic
neurotic tension, were slightly less exciting than Allen's more
complex works. Where the previous three films were based on one
fundamental idea, *Hannah and Her Sisters* marks a return to a
much more intricate narrative strategy, reflecting the complications of living in contemporary New York City, which, after all, is
what Allen is best at.

The film, which is divided into "chapters," each of which has its
own heading, opens with a Thanksgiving party at Hannah's apartment. Hannah's husband, Elliot, has a crush on Hannah's younger
sister Lee, a fact of which Lee is blushingly and demurely aware.
The third sister, Holly, embarrassedly asks Hannah to lend her
money so that she can start a catering business with a friend in
order to make a living in between cocaine trips and infrequent
acting jobs. Unlike her jittery family, Hannah seems completely

111

self-confident and in control, and she graciously consents to support Holly financially.

Elliot eventually manages to assure Lee that he and Hannah are growing apart. He feels unmanned by Hannah's self-reliance, he says, and wants someone who is more dependent. Lee leaves her depressive artist lover, Frederick, and starts an illicit love affair with Elliot.

Holly's catering business is extremely successful, but is nipped in the bud when her friend and partner, April, starts dating the attractive (and married) architect with whom Holly has been going out. Holly decides to give up her acting career and take up writing instead. Hannah lends her more money, but is mortified when she learns that Holly's first manuscript concerns a married couple reminiscent of herself and Elliot, and that some of the dialogue is taken word for word from her private conversations with her husband.

Holly meets Hannah's ex-husband, Mickey, a compulsive hypochondriac, at *Tower Records* and learns that his life has been even more traumatic than hers over the past few years. Mickey went to his doctor because of a slight loss of hearing in one ear and was terrified to learn that this might be the symptom of a brain tumor. (The only other time when something was actually wrong with him was when he and Hannah were told that he was infertile, and they decided to use Mickey's best friend—as usual played by Tony Roberts—as a sperm donor.)

After innumerable tests, the doctors conclude that Mickey does not have a brain tumor. Quite unexpectedly, however, he now enters a serious life crisis. Terrified by the thought of living in an absurd, godless universe, he quits his job as a television producer, tries to convert to Catholicism, and later to kill himself. After his unsuccessful suicide attempt, Mickey dazedly walks into the *Metro* movie theater which is playing the old Marx Brothers film, *Duck Soup*. While watching the movie, Mickey suddenly realizes the absurdity of obsessively searching for answers that one may never find. He decides to try to enjoy life more and snaps out of his depression. Now, one month later, he agrees to take a look at Holly's new manuscript, and the two of them start going out together.

At the end of the film, the family gets together for Thanksgiving at Hannah's house—two years after the party in the opening scene. Elliot has now realized how much he loves his wife; Lee has married her professor from Columbia University; and Holly and Mickey have married each other. Evan, the father of the three sisters, is playing *Isn't It Romantic* on the piano. In the final shot, an ecstatic looking Holly tells Mickey that she is pregnant. The tune changes to *I'm in Love Again,* Mickey embraces her, and the film ends.

Like most of Allen's films, *Hannah and Her Sisters* contains elements of a number of his other works. As we shall see, however, these elements are amalgamated in a much more satisfying manner here than in any of Allen's previous works. As in his earlier films, Allen has borrowed certain themes and narrative patterns from various classic works. The narrative strategy of switching between the points-of-view of various family members and Mickey has clear parallels to the one which Tolstoy used in *Anna Karenina.* We have already seen the influence of Tolstoy's novel in the analysis of *Love and Death* in chapter 3, and again it is illuminating to compare the Allen persona to Levin in that on the one hand we get an outside view of the family through his eyes, and on the other we are told the very moving story of his own complex emotional life.

The theme of the three sisters is of course well known from Chekhov's play as well as from Ingmar Bergman's film *Cries and Whispers.* Allen was clearly influenced by both works when he made *Interiors,* but *Interiors* seemed derivative and heavy-handed precisely because it was made more in the spirit of these classics than in the spirit of Allen himself. Because *Hannah and Her Sisters* is concerned with the typical Allenesque themes, and told with the typical Allenesque complexity, it succeeds where the previous family portrait failed.

We also see traces of Allen's previous works in the characters. Just as Annie Hall was not really the main character of her film, but the central event in the recent past of the main character, so this film is named for Hannah because she is the character around whom everybody else is centered, her sisters, her parents, her children, her husband, and her ex-husband. Very appropriately, her apartment is the setting for the three Thanksgiving parties which are so central to the story. She is also, as one critic said, the point at which "two triangles converge" when one sister has an affair with Hannah's husband and the other sister has one with her ex-husband.[2]

Hannah herself has certain characteristics in common with both Eve and Renata of *Interiors.* Like those two characters, Hannah has complete control of her own life and a genuine artistic talent. In fact, these very qualities cause *her* family—particularly her husband—to feel unmanned in her presence. Elliot's reason for falling in love with Hannah's sister, Lee, is that "I need someone I can matter to," and the morale of Holly's offensive manuscript is that Hannah is too "self-sufficient" and has "no needs." But as was the case with Eve, it is very clear to the audience that Hannah needs support and affection as much as her less self-confident family members.

Unlike Eve and Renata, however, Hannah also has the loving and life-giving traits of characters like Pearl and Tracy. She is extremely supportive of her family. In fact, in the scenes where Hannah has all her children around her, she calls to mind the nurturing mother figure of Isobel in *Stardust Memories*.[3] Hannah possesses generosity, sweetness, and kindness, and while all the other characters are confused, Hannah is calm and in control.

Mickey predictably has a number of characteristics in common with the former characters played by Allen himself. Visually the scenes of his tests are reminiscent of some of Allen's very early films, most significantly *Sleeper*. The extreme close-ups of the bespectacled face of the persona reveals to us his insecurity and vulnerability. In the earlier films, however, the things that threatened him were mostly external: hoods on the subway or scientists trying to remold his personality, evoking a slapstick atmosphere. In this film, the persona is threatened by a highly internal and not very amusing brain tumor.

Very surprisingly, however, we also find elements of the persona in Elliot. This seems even more striking because Elliot is played by British Michael Caine. In the extremely moving and embarrassingly recognizable scenes where he tries to get Lee's attention, we see him staging his own reality in a manner which is reminiscent of Allan Felix. In one early scene, the chapter heading of which is ". . . nobody, not even the rain, has such small hands," we see him running around frantically in SoHo (while on the soundtrack we hear Harry James playing *I've Heard That Song Before*) so that he can "accidentally" bump into Lee, "spontaneously" buy her a collection of e. e. cummings poetry, and tell her to read the one that reminds him of her, which he "happens to know" is on page 112.

Thematically we find a return to the obsessions of the Allen persona of the middle period. Mickey's acute awareness that eventually everybody is going to die "takes the pleasure out of everything," he tells Gail, a colleague at the television network. Like Boris, Alvy, Isaac, and Sandy, Mickey is not only scared of dying, but terrified by the idea of living in a hostile universe. He searches for answers at the library but comes up only with a not-very-helpful quotation from Tolstoy: "The only absolute knowledge attainable by man is that life is meaningless." Also like the earlier Allen characters he believes that "maybe love is the only answer."

After Mickey's attempted suicide, a complete and unexpected turnaround takes place. In Allen's earlier films we saw how the Allen persona's view of life was reflected in the films he went to see. In *Annie Hall,* Alvy repeatedly took Annie to see Marcel Ophul's four-and-a-half hour long documentary on the Nazis, *The Sorrow and the Pity.* In *Stardust Memories,* one of the central conflicts occurred when Isobel could not come with Sandy to see Vittorio De Sica's classic *The Bicycle Thief* because of her children. In *Hannah and Her Sisters,* the central epiphanic moment in Mickey's life is triggered not by a serious European film but by an old Marx Brothers movie, namely *Duck Soup.* The anarchic, irreverent zaniness of that movie suddenly makes Mickey realize how futile his obsession with death has been. And for the first time in all of Allen's career, he actually has his persona verbally renounce his obsession with death and the universe. As Mickey tells Holly:

> I started to feel how can you even think of killing yourself? . . . I mean, look at all the people up there on the screen. You know, they're real funny, and what if the worst *is* true? What if there's no God, and you only go around once and that's it? Well, you know, don't you want to be part of the experience? . . . And I'm thinking to myself, geez, I should stop ruining my life searching for answers I'm never gonna get, and just enjoy it while it lasts. And you know—after, who knows? . . . Maybe there *is* something. Nobody really knows. I know "maybe" is a very slim reed to hang your whole life on, but that's the best we have. And then I started to sit back, and I actually began to enjoy myself.

Mickey's new hopeful attitude is emphasized by the minor miracle that happens at the end of the film. Despite the fact that Mickey had been told by two doctors that he could never have children, Holly—to whom he is now married—joyously tells him that she is pregnant. In the context of this film and all of Allen's other works, we have to take for granted that Holly, like Tracy, is a trustworthy and dependable character, and that Mickey is indeed the father of the child she is expecting. What her pregnancy proves, then, is that keeping one's faith, in true *shlemiel*-fashion, is going to pay off in the end. In this film, the persona's despair over death and the expanding universe is finally replaced by hope for the future and the human race, as symbolized in the fact that

Holly is carrying his child. And, of course, the Allen persona never *did* believe in scientific evidence.[4]

At the time of the nationwide opening of *Hannah and Her Sisters,* Allen was already busy finishing the first shooting of his next feature film, *Radio Days.* Like *Zelig, Broadway Danny Rose,* and *The Purple Rose of Cairo, Radio Days* is an extremely enjoyable compendious miniature—a sort of thumbnail sketch of the golden days of the radio in the 1930s and 1940s. The voice-over narrator, Joe, collects old radio stories, and (in Woody Allen's voice) tells us anecdotes from his childhood about various radio celebrities, interchanged with tales of the members of his own family and the effect that the radio had on their lives. As in so many other Allen films, all the events that are recounted are obviously filtered through the consciousness and memory of the central character.

At the center of the film we have a dazzling array of meticulously cast characters, the most important of whom are the members of Joe's family. Much to the regret of Joe's father, they live in a house in Rockaway with Joe's maternal grandparents, his mother's sister Ceil, Ceil's husband Abe and their daughter Ruthie, and Mom and Ceil's sister Bea who desperately wants to get married.

Each one of these characters has a favorite program that he or she listens to vehemently and that to some extent reflects his or her character. Mom—while cleaning the dirty dishes—listens to the glamorous Broadway gossip in "Breakfast with Irene and Roger." Ceil, who is not too smart, listens to a ventriloquist despite the fact that, as Uncle Abe tells her, you cannot see whether or not he moves his lips.

Aunt Bea loves the music programs, and Joe tells us that thanks to her he still gets "instant memory flashes" whenever he hears certain tunes. We then cut to a somewhat unexpected and hilariously stylized flash which is obviously filtered through Joe's memory. Whenever he hears *Mairzy Doats,* he is reminded of the incident when Mister Zipsky, who was normally such a quiet man, had a nervous breakdown and ran amuck in his underwear with a meat cleaver.

More important in terms of the typical Allen universe are the programs that Joe himself and Uncle Abe listen to. Joe's favorite radio personality is "The Masked Avenger," a mysterious punisher of criminals who flies over the rooftops of Manhattan shouting "Beware evildoers wherever you are!" Joe imagines that he looks like "a cross between Superman and Cary Grant." And in fact, Joe's fascination with "The Masked Avenger" echoes the various Superman stories that Allen has used all through his career. In the Heywood Allen days the persona already told the audience that he identified with Superman because both of them had a habit of undressing in telephone booths. Conversely, Allen's films have often been a revolt against what one might call "The Superman Syndrome."

Another interesting thing about "The Masked Avenger" is the fact that later in life Joe learns that the actor whose voice was used for the part was a short, balding, middle-aged man—played by the actor Wallace Shawn. In *Manhattan*, Mary was constantly telling a very annoyed Ike about her sexy and brilliant ex-husband, Jeremiah. When the two of them accidentally ran into Jeremiah in a clothing store, he, too, turned out to be played by the same not-so-gorgeous-looking Wallace Shawn.

Uncle Abe likes to listen to "Bill Kearn's Sports Legends." The episode of that program which Joe recounts to us is also clearly exaggerated and distorted by the passage of time. It deals with one Kirby Kyle, pitcher for the St. Louis Cardinals. Kyle loses a leg in a hunting accident but continues pitching regardlessly because "he had heart." Then he loses his right arm, which fortunately is not his pitching arm, and later he goes blind. Through it all he continues because he has "instinct and heart." When he is finally killed by a truck, he wins eighteen games in the "big league in the sky."

The Kirby Kyle character calls to mind Danny Rose's clients, the one-armed juggler, the one-legged tap-dancer, and the stuttering ventriloquist, but he also calls to mind Danny Rose himself. Like a number of Allen's works, Kyle's story reflects a concern with and sympathy for characters who have "heart" and courage to continue their struggle regardless of the blows that life deals them—although it does so in a tongue-in-cheek fashion. Danny Rose is, as we have seen, the epitome of this kind of character. Furthermore, Kyle in a sense reflects the character of Uncle Abe himself—he refuses to give up. Despite the naggings of his wife, Abe continues to bring home the multitude of fish that his friends at Sheepshead Bay give him whenever he visits. Abe is not as gentle as Danny Rose and the classical *shlemiel* though. Whenever Ceil complains about having to fillet all the fish, he tells her to "take the gas pipe."

In between the narrative about Joe's family, we are presented with the fairy tale of Sally White, the blond floozy from Brooklyn whose dream of a career in radio comes true. (Again, as in *Broadway Danny Rose,* Mia Farrow is absolutely hilarious as the dumb blonde with the shrill voice.) At the beginning of the film, Sally works at the King Cole Room nightclub as a cigarette girl. She is having an affair with Roger (of Mom's favorite program "Break-fast with Irene and Roger") who is "exploding with desire" every time he sees her. Sally takes the importunate Roger to the roof of the King Cole Room. After they have finished their business and a thunderstorm breaks out, they find that the door opens from the inside only, so they cannot get off the roof. "And that," Joe informs us, "is exactly how it happened!" The story tells that Roger was then hit by lightning and was absent from the "Breakfast" pro-gram for a month. Another version, Joe tells us, claims that the door was finally opened from the inside by Irene who had brought an exotic Latin playboy to the roof with the same inten-tion as her husband. As usual in Allen's works, we are warned that any allegations that "that is exactly how it happened" has to be taken with at least one grain of salt.

Before the film even begins, its playful mood is suggested by Harry James's odd arrangement of Nikolai Rimsky-Korsakov's *Flight of the Bumble Bee* which is played over the credits. Again, reflecting a central element in his works, Allen very cleverly uses a piece of music which inherently juxtaposes nineteenth-century European highbrow culture with a twentieth-century American popular culture. Then Joe's adult voice over an almost dark screen—the darkness is broken only by flashlights—starts telling us the story of the time when two burglars robbed the house of the Needlemans, Joe's neighbors. In the middle of the looting, the telephone rings. In order not to wake up the entire neigh-borhood, the burglars decide to answer it, only to find that they are on the air on the "Guess that Tune" contest. Between them they manage to guess the three tunes—the first one ironically is *Dancing in the Dark*—and win the "Grand Jackpot." As a result, the next day a gigantic truck pulls up in front of the robbed Nee-dleman house, loaded with new furniture and refrigerators galore.

Thus, the medium of the radio is continually seen as a motivat-ing force. Throughout the film, the indication is that, like it or not, the various characters are very much influenced by it, the glamorous performers as well as the ordinary people who listen to them, and almost everything that happens in their lives is related to the radio. When Roger cannot leave Irene and marry Sally, the reason is that "our ratings are too high." Joe's father is so embar-rassed by his inability to live up to the "American Dream" that he refuses to tell his family what he does for a living. The only reason why Joe ever finds out that his father is a taxi driver is that he has to pick up their radio at the repair shop. It is very heavy and Joe cannot carry it home so he has to take a taxi. Guess who the driver is!

In the course of the film, Joe gets pummeled innumerable times, and always in connection with the radio. Once when the family meet one of the radio "Whiz Kids" at the zoo, his father smacks him because he is not a genius. Another time Joe has stolen the funds collected for a "Jewish homeland in Palestine" so that he can buy a "Masked Avenger Secret Compartment Ring." His parents are called in to see the rabbi who is very disappointed in him. The reason why Joe did this, his mother assures the rabbi, is that "every night he listens to the radio. I can't keep him away." The rabbi is obviously worried by this because listening to the radio "tends to induce bad values, false dreams, lazy habits." Joe tries to pacify the upset rabbi by calling him "My faithful Indian companion," and immediately the three adults start thrashing away at the poor child to prove to each other that they are not "too lenient." Toward the end of the film, Pop actually stops spanking Joe because the sad and moving broadcast of Polly Phelps—an eight-year-old girl who falls down a well—starts on the radio.

When Bea's many dates go wrong, a radio is often involved. Once a very promising suitor breaks down and cries because *I'm Getting Sentimental over You* is played on the radio and reminds him of his dead fiancée, Leonard! Bea immediately realizes that he is not the right man for her.

For radio buffs one of the most hilarious moments of the film occurs when Bea is asked out by the attractive and boisterous Mr. Manulis. On the way home from a lovely evening at Coney Island, they run out of gas and are stranded on the tip of Breezy Point. Mr. Manulis seems quite happy about the situation, and Bea seems not to mind too much either. They turn on the radio, but the seductive tango music is interrupted by a special news bulletin which declares that "the landing of hundreds of unidentified spacecrafts has now been officially confirmed as a full-scale invasion of the earth by Martians." This is, of course, a homage to Orson Welles's famous Mercury Theatre production of H. G. Wells's *War of the Worlds,* which was broadcast on October 30, 1938 as a Halloween prank. Terrified by the approaching Martians, the not-so-chivalrous Mr. Manulis panics, runs off, and leaves poor Bea behind.

What is suggested is that, whether we like it or not, the radio (and by implication the younger media) is not just an adventitious piece of furniture or source of entertainment, but a phenomenon which is very much an integral part of our lives, and plays an important role in defining our character. Again, as in Allen's earlier films, we, the audience of *Radio Days,* are implicated in this intimation.

The last scene of the film takes place on New Years Eve of 1943. We are at the King Cole Room where a big New Year party is taking place. All the familiar faces are there, including Sally, who now has a beautifully modulated voice, with her date, The Masked Avenger. One new character is the singer, Monica Charles, who sings a very quiet version of *You'd Be So Nice to Come Home To.* From focusing on Monica we cut to Bea who has not been able to get a date, and thus sits at home, listening to the radio. What she hears is Monica Charles and the transmission of the New Year party at the King Cole Room. The rest of the scene is cross-edited between the two different worlds, bringing them together.

At this point in the film, as at the end of *Stardust Memories,* we are reminded of the fact that we, too, are an audience watching both layers of the fiction. The fact that the cameo role of Monica is played by Allen's ex-woman friend and leading lady, Diane Keaton, only serves to emphasize this feeling of momentary bewilderment and disillusion. In his wonderful book on the shooting of *Radio Days,* which in itself is a very valuable document on filmmaking, Thierry de Navacelle comments on the filming of this scene which Mia Farrow, Allen's present woman friend and leading lady, witnessed in "civilian" clothes. "It is strange and fascinating to see Monica Charles and Sally at the same time. They're so different, especially today, with Monica's white dress and Sally's baggy clothes."[5]

The very ending of the film stresses our involvement even more. As midnight approaches, Sally buys cigarettes from the new cigarette girl at the King Cole Room. (Very amusingly she buys "Lucky Strike".) She is reminded of old times, her voice momentarily slipping back into its old shrillness, and tells her new friends of the beautiful view from the roof. They all decide to go up there and immediately we jump to the conclusion that probably they will all be stuck there, the way that Sally and Roger were at the beginning. Having watched 1944 come in, they get sentimental and start wondering whether future generations will ever hear about them. It starts raining and they decide to go back down, and to our surprise they manage to open the door with no problems. "The Masked Avenger" shouts his famous sign-off— "Beware evil-doers wherever you are!"—the door locks, and we suddenly realize that in fact *we* are the ones who are stuck on the roof—indefinitely!

The implication that art affects real life is thus as clear in this film as in Allen's earlier films. Again, as in, for instance, *Annie Hall*, we are completely willing to accept the events of the film as "real life" and the characters as "real people." There are, however, a few instances where the influence works the other way around so that "real life" affects art. When Aunt Bea and her date Sy take Joe to a radio show, "The Silver Dollar Jackpot," Bea is chosen as a contestant. Because of Uncle Abe's passion for fish, Bea chooses that as her topic, and the show is thus marked by the life of Joe's family. Similarly, as Thierry de Navacelle tells us in his book, the filming of *Radio Days* itself was influenced by real life. Because Dianne Wiest (who plays Bea) had to go to her father's funeral during the reshoot, Woody Allen came up with and filmed a whole new sequence in which Sally is kidnapped by the gangster Rocco. Instead of killing her, Rocco decides to have his cousin Angelo ask someone an "unrefusable favor," and that becomes the first step to Sally's stardom within the radio.

More than anything else, *Radio Days* is a sentimental journey back to the glory days of the radio as well as through several of Allen's own works. A number of the scenes contain a tender melancholia and beauty, unequalled in any other Allen film. The dwellingly slow scene where Aunt Bea and her date Chester (played by Allen's sound mixer James Sabat who has worked with him since *Bananas*) take Joe to Radio City Music Hall is completely exhilarating. The beautiful, golden photography certainly helps to emphasize the mood of the film, and very much carries the stamp of a man who has a vast experience within his field, namely director of photography Carlo Di Palma. Di Palma began his career in 1942 as a focus operator on Luchino Visconti's *Ossessione*, the film which marked the "birth" of Italian neorealism. He also worked with Allen on *Hannah and Her Sisters*.

In addition to the many references to Allen's old films, a number of his old "repertory" players are seen in cameo roles. Diane Keaton, as mentioned, appears as a singer, Tony Roberts plays Max, the emcee of "The Silver Dollar Jackpot." (All through *Annie Hall*, Alvy and his friend Rob—the role played by Tony Roberts—call each other Max. Apparently Woody Allen and Tony Roberts have done the same ever since.) Jeff Daniels—who played Tom Baxter in *The Purple Rose of Cairo*—plays radio G-man Biff Baxter. Danny Aiello, who played Cecilia's husband Monk in the same film, plays her abductor Rocco in this one. Rocco's mother (Gina DeAngelis) also played the mother of the mobsters in *Broadway Danny Rose*. For all these reasons, *Radio Days* is probably Allen's most nostalgic film. As the adult Joe says at the beginning of the film: "Now it's all gone 'cept for the memories."

In the epilogue of his book, Thierry de Navacelle tells us that in December 1986, before the release of *Radio Days,* Woody Allen was already finishing the shooting of his next film at the Astoria Studios in Queens. "A big house has been built in the middle of the sound stage," de Navacalle tells us, "and Mia Farrow, Dianne Wiest, and Sam Shepard are working on a scene."[6] The film in question was, of course, *September.* And in 1987, despite the fact that the entire project was eventually completely redone, and Shepard does not appear in the final version of the film, Allen, who for over a decade had had one picture released every single year, for the first time in his career had two new films out in one year. It would later prove not to be the last time.

Like *A Midsummer Night's Sex Comedy, September* is set in a house in the country and has six central characters who undergo various changes in the course of the film. As Stephanie, one of these characters, says: "We are all up here, isolated from the world. Unpredictable things happen." But apart from these superficial similarities, *September* has absolutely nothing in common with Allen's other "country" film. In fact, in terms of its mood and the central concern of the mother-daughter relationship, it is much more reminiscent of Allen's first "serious" film *Interiors* and of Ingmar Bergman's *Autumn Sonata.* Like the mother character in Bergman's film, Diane is a celebrity whose self-absorption and self-reliance has left her daughter Lane emotionally crippled.

After an attempted suicide, Lane has spent several months in the family house in Vermont where she has fallen in love with Peter, a would-be writer who rents her guest cottage, while Howard, a middle-aged, worldly-wise English widower has fallen in love with her. At the time we enter this universe, Diane and her new husband Lloyd, who is a physicist, have arrived for a visit, and Lane's friend Stephanie is there to get away from her husband and children for a while.

The music, as usual in Allen's films, plays an important part in *September,* and over the opening titles we hear a lovely piano version of Frank Loesser's *On a Slow Boat to China.*[7] This tune later becomes associated with Stephanie who plays it to entertain the others when the electricity goes off during a thunderstorm. After the opening titles, we get a dwelling traveling shot through the beautiful and seemingly peaceful house. On the sound track we hear a voice speaking astonishingly in French about being in the country and loving it: "J'aime beaucoup des choses à la campagne.

J'aime les fleurs. J'aime les arbres." This surprising opening statement to a Woody Allen film is spoken by Stephanie, who is practicing her French with Howard who is a teacher of that language.

When Lane enters from the garden a few moments later, we are presented with one of the film's main concerns: at age fourteen, Lane ostensibly shot her mother's gangster lover. Diane is "a survivor," Lane tells Peter. "She went on with her life, but I got stuck with the nightmares." The fact that Diane is now trying to persuade Peter to write her biography brings these old conflicts between the vibrant and vigorous mother and the insecure, broken-down daughter to the surface again. And contradicting our first impression of the house itself, we soon learn that underneath the peaceful exterior, things are quite different from what they seem.

Diane is apparently the sanguine, life-giving, and exuberant successor of characters like Annie Hall, Pearl, and Tracy. She is full of energy and wonderful stories of her eventful life, and at one point she finds and plays with an old ouija board which seems to represent the "magic" we know from Allen's other works. Her husband, Lloyd, has inherited obvious traits from the later Allen persona. Through his profession he has realized that the universe is "haphazard, morally neutral, and unimaginably violent," that "it does not matter one way or the other" because "it's all random" and will eventually vanish forever, and that "all space, all time are just temporary convulsions." The only thing that keeps him going, he tells Peter, is Diane who is "warm and vital" and can hold him at night.

If, however, we pay attention to what we are told about Diane indirectly, we see the dark side of her character. Thus, in addition to being a survivor, a quality which in the Allenesque universe we are used to admiring, Diane is also a killer, as seen in her tendency to exterminate all things around her, particularly things that belong to her daughter. She constantly picks Lane's flowers but does not bother putting them in water and instead leaves them all over the house to die. When Lane, as a last resort to build a life for herself, decides to sell the house, Diane whimsically decides that she and Lloyd want to live there. She is not only completely unsympathetic toward Lane's very real financial difficulties, but also reveals that she has decided to replace the pond with a swimming pool. She has always hated the pond, she says, because "there's live things in there." Lloyd proudly goes on to tell everybody that Diane is a wonderful swimmer, which emphasizes the fact that she, as opposed to Lane, is a survivor.

Furthermore, Diane is perfectly willing to make money on a biography, even if it means putting Lane through the trauma of the shooting scandal again. She cannot leave the incident out of the book, she says, because that is what "everybody wants to hear." She reveals herself as a vulture, literally feeding on her daughter, earning her sustenance through Lane's misery. This is confirmed even further when during their final confrontation over the house, Lane defiantly blurts out their dark secret: it was Diane herself, not Lane, who killed the gangster lover. Ever since childhood, Lane has been a scapegoat, enabling Diane to continue her carefree way of life.

In the last scene Diane suddenly leaves in order to avoid further confrontation; she distributes trinkets among Lane and Stephanie as if they were little children and she the fairy godmother. When she struts out of the house, we hear her guffawing that she still travels with her diaphragm which is "like a lucky charm" to her. This emblem of her character stresses her double role once more. Like the previous female *shlemiel* characters, she seems exuberant and life-giving, but is in actuality quite the opposite in that her voluptuousness and epicureanism prevents both actual and potential children from living. This is, of course, also reflected in her name, which in addition to being the name of two of Allen's most compelling leading ladies (Diane Keaton and Dianne Wiest), is the name of the ancient Roman goddess of the hunt.

After Diane and Lloyd are gone, Lane complains that "now she's off to Palm Beach as though nothing had happened." In fact, their departure calls to mind the ending of F. Scott Fitzgerald's *The Great Gatsby* when the narrator, Nick Carraway, tells us what "they were careless people, Tom and Daisy—they smashed up things and creatures and then retreated . . . and let other people clean up the mess they had made."[8] Both Diane and Lloyd are totally unheeding of the fact that everyone else is completely devastated, each for his or her own reason. The similarity is further emphasized by the fact that the role of Peter in this film is played by Sam Waterston who played Nick in the 1976 Jack Clayton film version of *The Great Gatsby*.[9] Also, during the thunderstorm, while we focus on Diane playing with her ouija board and summoning all her departed lovers, we hear Stephanie playing Irving Berlin's *What'll I Do* on the piano. That same tune had a central function in the Jack Clayton film.

Allen's first "serious" film, *Interiors*, was criticized as being too theatrical and Bergmanesque for its own good. The same could be said of *September*, all of which takes place inside the house. Its dialogue at times seems stilted, and the character of Lane (like the Liv Ullmann character in *Autumn Sonata*) is terribly enervating in her self-pity. Thus, although you really try to be sympathetic toward her, at times you are reminded of a central motif in *Take the Money and Run!*, and you catch yourself wanting to take off her glasses and step on them. One serious problem in this connection lies in the fact that it is difficult in comparison to really be angry with Diane despite all the damage she causes. In fact, one actually laughs when she hurts Lane with remarks such as, "You dress like a Polish refugee." Also, like Bergman, Allen often uses his familiar "repertory players." The best and most moving scenes in *September* are those portraying the beginning relationship between Peter and Stephanie, and the success of these scenes is very much due to the acting of and chemistry between Dianne Wiest and Sam Waterston.

As in all Allen's later films, shared cultural and culinary pleasures play an important role. Thus from the moment at the very beginning of the film when we hear that Peter has given Stephanie an Art Tatum and Ben Webster record, we know that his relationship with Lane is in danger. This impression is strengthened when Lane's plans for her and Peter to go and see a Kurosawa film fall through. Furthermore, the importance of the feelings that Peter and Stephanie have for each other is illustrated visually in the scene when it is finally brought to fruition, and we see them filmed in profile, holding their arms and heads so that they form the shape of a heart.

Peter's role and its function are reminiscent of the role that Sam Waterston played in *Interiors* and the one he would later play in *Crimes and Misdemeanors*. He represents poetry and human dignity amidst all the turmoil and suffering. When Lloyd, the physicist, tells him about the hopelessly haphazard universe, Peter's response is: "You feel so sure of that when you look out on a clear night like tonight and see all those millions of stars that none of it matters?" He is writing a novel about survival (the main reason why he is interested in Diane's life), and in an early scene he tells Stephanie about his book. He is planning to call it *The History Professor,* a title referring to his father who was blacklisted during the McCarthy era and who supported the familiy by playing poker and betting on horses. The father fits in somewhere between *The Front* and *Broadway Danny Rose* it would seem. He is, in terms of the Allen code, a person to be admired for surviving the blacklisting in the typical New York fashion worthy of a Damon Runyon character. In the final analysis, the saddest thing in the film is not so much Lane's terrible problems, with which one has trouble identifying, but the fact that Peter decides to give up his book and go back to writing "beer commercials and deodorant ads" on Madison Avenue.

In the same scene, Stephanie tells Peter an extremely moving story about a young man she fell in love with in Paris when she was young. He did not speak any English and "we spent a summer together trying to make each other understand our feelings. The funny thing was that it didn't matter that we only knew a few words." All through the film, a lot of emphasis is put on Stephanie. She speaks the first line of dialogue in the film—saying in French that she loves so many things about the country. In the last scene she makes us aware that the title of the film refers not to the month when it takes place but rather to the future: "In a few days it'll be September." She also gets to speak the final line, trying to reassure Lane—and us—that "It's gonna be okay!"

Toward the end of the film, almost all the characters have been jilted: Peter by Stephanie, Lane by Peter, and Howard by Lane. They are all brokenhearted—even Stephanie who has made the decision to give up Peter and go back to her humdrum life in Philadelphia. But although the song that opens the film would thus fit any character in it (they would all desperately "love to get" somebody "on a slow boat to China"), it is really Stephanie's song. She is the one who plays it on the piano, and in the indomitable, dreamlike spirit of the *shlemiel,* she, despite all the bleakness, expresses confident feelings about and hope for the past (the story about the boy in Paris), the present ("J'aime beaucoup des choses à la campagne!"), and the future "Its gonna be okay!"

In the very last scene, she puts on her record, indicating to us that Peter and what he represents will not be forgotten. She makes herself a cup of tea and sits down at the kitchen table with Lane. After that, we leave the same way we came in, with a long traveling shot through the house, past a "still life" on the display case of all the photographs of Diane and the booze bottles that have come to be associated with her, finally closing on the image of the hallway, while on the sound track we hear Stephanie's record of *My Ideal.*

The pretitle sequence of Allen's next film, *Another Woman,* is the reverse mirror image of this closing shot. The first person retrospective narrator and central character introduces herself and her world. She has entered her fifties not too long ago, and, she tells us, has "achieved a decent measure of fulfillment, both professionally and personally." Her name is Marion Post, she is director of undergraduate studies in philosophy at a "very fine women's college," and she is married to Ken, a successful cardiologist. What we see during this voice-over opening is a shot of a long hallway—with a number of doors on each side—through which Marion enters, followed by a group of displayed photographs of Marion's family which she introduces to us.

She has just started writing a book, and because of the noise from construction work in her building, she has sublet a small apartment. On her first day there, she realizes that due to some "acoustical oddness" she can overhear intimate conversations from the office of a psychiatrist next door. She tries to block out the sound with large pillows so that she can work, but while she is napping during the afternoon, one of the pillows slips down, and Marion wakes up and hears the sad and anguished voice of a young woman who talks of a dream in which she realized that "deception" has become a very dominant feature in her life. It was, the young woman says, "as if a curtain had parted and I could see myself clearly. And I was afraid of what I saw." When the woman leaves, Marion peeks through the door and sees that she is pregnant.

Marion finds that she is haunted by the young woman's words and through the rest of the film she is forced by a number of unrelated coincidences to examine all areas of her life, and she realizes that self-deception is very much a part of her own existence as well. Her sister-in-law tells her that she is "deluding" herself about her relationship with her brother Paul: "Of course in a way he idolizes you . . . he also hates you." On examining the belongings of her mother who died recently, Marion has to admit to herself that whereas *she* was allowed to finish her education, Paul was forced to work in a paper-box factory. Once, when she follows the young woman through dark alleys, Marion bumps into her old friend Claire, whom she has not seen for years, and who is now a moderately successful actress. During a brief conversation over a drink with Claire and her husband, Marion learns that her friend both envies and despises her for her dishonesty and unconscious role-playing. "You," Claire tells her, "should be the actress."

Marion is finally forced to admit that her husband is having an affair with her best friend, that her apparently self-confident and successful father regards his life as a complete failure, and that by deciding to have an abortion during her first marriage, she was responsible for the death of the unborn child as well as part of herself. She also reexperiences the anger of her first husband, Sam, when she told him of her abortion, and his self-inflicted death many years later.

When the young woman in the psychiatrist's office wonders whether she made the right choice when she married her husband rather than "someone else" she once knew, Marion is reminded of Larry Lewis, a warm and passionate man who tried to persuade her not to marry his aloof and unfeeling friend, Ken. Marion gradually comes to understand that maybe her life has been too cerebral and lacking real passion. During one of the young woman's sessions next door, Marion imagines how Ken's perceptive young daughter Laura, who is also Marion's friend, would describe her to her boyfriend: "She sort of stands above people and evaluates them." When her brother Paul in the past showed her something he had written, Marion dismissed it as being "too emotional." "To the objective observer," she tells him, "it's so embarrassing." After Marion has finally met and talked with the young woman, she hears herself described to the psychiatrist: "She can't allow herself to feel, so the result is she's led this cold, cerebral life and, has alienated everyone around her."

While the Allen persona is not very strongly represented in this film, *Another Woman* very much deals with the original and the extended Jungian meaning of the word "persona." In the classical Roman and Greek theater, the persona was a mask worn by the actor, representing the role he played. Jung uses the term to refer to the public face we put on, the role we choose to play due to various pressures from our surroundings, at the risk, Jung says, of becoming identical with that persona. Both of these related definitions of the term are represented in the film.

Several times Marion sees a white mask in her mind's eye. Once it is situated outside the cage of a black panther, referring to a poem, "The Panther," by Rainer Maria Rilke, which Marion finds among her mother's possessions. During a flashback to her marriage with Sam, we learn that Marion gave the white mask to him as a present. It was all, she tells him, that she could "afford from that great store." It was originally made for a French production of *La Gioconda*, and is, in other words, a theatrical mask. In addition, of course, the film deals with Marion discovering her own self-deception and finally deciding to remove her mask, her persona. The use of Rilke's poetry is important in this respect in that it often deals with the existential quest for a spiritual identity. The other Rilke poem, which we are presented with, is her mother's favorite, "Archaic Torso of Apollo." Marion reads the final line, which is streaked by her mother's tears: "For here there is no place that does not see you. You must change your life." Thus, whereas the title can obviously be seen as referring to the fact that Marion finds out that Ken has someone else, or the fact that it is the voice of the young woman which prompts her to reexamine her life, the final result of her involuntary probing is that underneath the self-delusive "mask" she has been wearing, she discovers a different Marion, another woman.

As in a number of Allen's films, it is obvious that what we see is not necessarily to be taken at face value, but is often filtered through the mind of the central character. Thus when we look back at her past, it is not in neutral flashbacks, as illustrated in a number of instances where Marion appears in the past in her present shape, or as in the scene where during the discussion with Sam about her abortion, she changes back and forth between the young Marion and the middle-aged Marion.

Similarly, a great part of the film is meant to be understood symbolically. We repeatedly see Marion walking through long empty hallways. From the very beginning, it is thus suggested that what we follow is really Marion's unconscious, and indeed Freudian symbolism, and particularly the interpretation of dreams, plays an important role in the film. Thus, the young woman first appears when Marion is asleep. When she, or her voice, pops up, it either seems as if Marion wills it and conjures her up, or she constitutes parts of Marion's dreams. Her problems are so similar to Marion's that one gets the feeling that she represents a part of Marion's own personality.

Once Marion follows her down dark, empty streets and is led to her old friend Claire, and in a central scene she meets the young woman in a cavernous, dreamlike, and dusty antique store. Marion has been walking around the city trying to find an anniversary present for Ken when she suddenly discovers the shop. She enters and mysteriously finds it completely empty. In the background she hears music. She looks at all the objects on display, most of which are odd figures, art nouveau lamps, and stained glass pictures. Suddenly she hears muffled sounds, and she sees the young woman who is crying, looking at a reproduction of Gustav Klimt's famous painting *Hope* which portrays a naked, pregnant woman.

In an earlier scene, Marion and Ken go to a concert with Lydia (the woman with whom Ken is having an affair) and her husband Mark. What they hear is Gustav Mahler's *Fourth Symphony*. After the concert, a woman in a restaurant tells Marion that she is an ex-student of hers, and that Marion changed her life with her brilliant lectures on "ethics and moral responsibility."

Along with Freud and Mahler (among many others), Klimt, of course, belongs in Vienna at the turn of the century—a period which was very much marked by transition and upheavals. Whether or not the constant references to the various arts and sciences of this particular period are conscious on Allen's part, they do reflect some of the concerns of this and other Allen films. Thus Klimt's paintings—mirroring Marion's dilemma—constitute a kind of bridge between the strictly disciplined forms of the late nineteenth-century art nouveau and the early twentieth-century expressionism, the aim of which was to depict emotions by means of distortion.

The music of Gustav Mahler is likewise schismatical, being influenced partly by the harmonic language of Richard Wagner and Franz Liszt and partly by the simplicity and directness of folk music. In Mahler's music, as in Allen's films, we find an unexpected and exhilarating mixture of highbrow and popular culture. The fourth movement of the *Fourth Symphony* consists of verses from *Des Knaben Wunderhorn,* an anthology of German folk verse, and describes a child's view of the culinary and musical pleasures in Heaven: "Fine apples, fine pears and fine grapes. . . . If you want venison or hare, down the open streets they come running. . . . There is no music on earth that can be compared to ours," etc. The childish rapture and rattling off calls to mind the ending of *Manhattan* where Isaac enumerates the things that make life worth living, among them Mozart's *Jupiter Symphony,* "Louis Armstrong's recording of *Potatohead Blues,*" "those incredible apples and pears by Cezanne," and "the crabs at Sam Wo's."

The fact that the art of this period marked the birth of the new century, inherently containing elements of both nineteenth-century culture and what would come to characterize twentieth-century culture, plays an important part. As usual in Allen's work, the music is used to illustrate the characters. Thus when Marion is with her father, what is played is Bach, and when she is with Larry Lewis, we hear an instrumental version of *A Fine Romance.* When they are kissing passionately, the corresponding lyrics, had they been there, would have said "we should be like a couple of hot tomatoes," and, when Marion pushes Larry away, "but you're as cold as yesterday's mashed potatoes." Very significantly, most of the art used in this film contains a contrast within itself: the contrast between rigidity and the emotional in Klimt, between the classical and the popular in Mahler, and between European and American art in Kurt Weill whose *Bilbao Song* is used repeatedly.

In Allen's earlier films, as we have seen, there was a tendency to sharply divide the characters into the emotional, those representing the heart, and the intellectual, those representing the brain.

Another Woman, mirroring the art that is used in it, marks a subtle but important change in that respect. The characters in this film often contain both aspects of the former dichotomy, and neither aspect is seen as good or bad in and of itself. Ken, Marion's husband, illustrates the worst combination of the two in that he is the cold and cerebral heart specialist. Larry Lewis on the other hand represents the ideal, the kindhearted, and passionate intellectual.

Over a decade ago, after Allen had turned forty, his friend Marshall Brickman, in answer to a question about Allen's psychological state, said: "The happy/unhappy axis is a fallacy in contemporary society. The point is to be awake, alert, functioning."[10] Thus in Allen's films of the late 1970s, being productive and intelligent, although that often led to neuroses or anhedonia, was preferable to happiness which usually entailed imbecility. Now Woody Allen, like Marion Post, has recently entered his fifties, and having come to terms with a number of the obsessions he introduced in *Love and Death* and *Annie Hall,* he has apparently found a new concern. Rather than drawing a sharp dividing line between the heart and the brain, or those who are intelligent and those who are happy, he now seems anxious to try to achieve a balance of the two within the individual. Trying to achieve happiness, in addition to being intelligent, is thus a very valid endeavor.

The concept of pregnancy and childbearing, as opposed to Marion's abortion, has an important symbolic function in the film. When Marion says that she has never quite "recovered my balance since turning fifty," one inevitably draws parallels to Allen himself and his own turning fifty a few years ago. Also, echoes of Alvy Singer, who told us that he had just turned forty, come to mind. Marion continues to tell the young woman that "Maybe it would be nice to have a child." In Marion's dream, Larry tells her that having a little girl has been the "greatest, most beautiful experience of my life." Meanwhile the camera focuses on the young, pregnant woman, played by Mia Farrow who was actually, I believe, carrying Allen's own first child at the time the film was shot. Consequently, there are various reasons to assume that some of Marion's concerns reflect Woody Allen's own thoughts over the past couple of years, and of all Allen's attempts at making a serious film, *Another Woman,* perhaps for that very reason, is easily the most moving and the most satisfying.

At the end of the film, Marion has apparently left Ken, and has obviously found a new balance in her life. She decides to tell the psychiatrist next door about the "accoustical oddness" so that it can be fixed, and when she asks him how she can get in touch with the young woman, he tells her that she has "gone away." Marion is now completely alone with her own conscious mind, at the beginning of a new, more fulfilling life. Her work, we are told, goes well, and on a sunny morning she decides to look through Larry's novel which has a character, Helenka, who is based on her. Larry's narrator tells of how he bumps into his best friend's future wife with whom he is in love. They stroll through Central Park and when a storm breaks, they "duck into an underpath" (again an unambiguous Freudian symbol as well as an allusion to *Manhattan*) to get out of the rain. They start kissing, but suddenly Helenka pushes him away. "But," the narrator says, "it was too late, because I now knew that she was capable of intense passion, if she would one day just allow herself to feel."

When Marion closes the book she feels both "wistfulness and hope"—the last being the title of the Klimt painting, and, as we find out only when we see the end titles, the name of the young, pregnant woman. The film ends with some of the most beautiful lines in any Allen movie: "I wondered if a memory is something you have or something you've lost. For the first time in a long time I felt at peace."

In 1989 Woody Allen, who for some time has been known as an almost frantically productive filmmaker, for the second time in his career had two films out in one year. The first of these, "Oedipus Wrecks" was part of a trilogy of short features, which are supposed to form a composite picture of Allen's native city, called *New York Stories*. The story which starts this film is a breathtaking portrayal of a neoexpressionist artist, directed by the ever-brilliant Martin Scorsese. The second is an annoying and insulting mess of a childish fantasy directed by Francis Coppola, based on a script by his young daughter. The story that ends the film, Allen's contribution, seems almost like a pastiche of his earlier works, particularly the short stories.

"Oedipus Wrecks" deals with one Sheldon Mills, formerly Millstein, and his immensely troubled relationship with his elderly mother. The film begins with a close-up of Woody Allen who, looking us straight in the eye, states: "I'm fifty years old. I'm a partner in a big law firm, you know, I'm very successful. And I still haven't resolved my relationship with my mother." We cut to a psychiatrist with whom we now realize Sheldon is sharing his oedipal agonies, but for a minute we have an eerie sensation that what we witnessed was Alvy Singer ten years later—the character who, a little over a decade ago, opened *Annie Hall* by confessing to us that he was going through a life crisis because he had just turned forty.

Sheldon's mother, Sadie Millstein, does not approve of his plans to marry Lisa, a *shiksa* who works in an advertising firm. "Where," she asks him, "do you come to a blonde with three children? What are you, an astronaut?" One day during a Sunday outing with Lisa and the children, a magician accidentally makes Sadie disappear, and she eventually turns up miraculously projected against the sky over Manhattan where she insists on discussing Sheldon's marriage plans and childhood bed-wetting with the various passersby. Only when her son decides that he has fallen in love with Treva Marx, a nice Jewish psychic who has been trying to help him solve the mystery, does she agree to come down.

When "Oedipus Wrecks" came out, many critics were ludicrously relieved that Allen had once again returned to the safe realm of comedy after no less than two "serious" films, and this short feature got rave reviews. Nevertheless it is not nearly as moving or surprising as *Another Woman*. Although it is a sweet little story, it is at times quite boring because it is concocted from material that Allen has used before.

The basic idea of using a magic box to project people was used in "The Kugelmass Episode," Allen's award winning story. The trick of the magician's box is that, like Little Joe's Masked Avenger ring, it has a secret compartment. Also as in "The Kugelmass Episode," it is on the advice of his psychiatrist that Sheldon goes to see someone who deals with "unexplained phenomena. Mysteries that science can't fathom." As in for instance *Annie Hall*, the New Yorkers are only too happy to stop and offer their opinions on anything Sadie tells them. Likewise several of the jokes are old and worn. When he cannot conjure up Sadie, the magician says to Sheldon, "Anything happens to your mother, I'll give you two free tickets to any show." This joke is a variation on Danny Rose's reply to an elderly man whose wife one of Danny's hopeless clients has hypnotized and cannot wake up, only what Danny Rose promised was a meal at any Chinese restaurant in New York.

This use of bathetic juxtaposition, which runs through all of "Oedipus Wrecks," we know from Allen's early works. At one point Sheldon gets so sick of his mother's constant hovering over his head that he tries to commit suicide by wetting his finger and thrusting it into a lamp socket. This is a visualization of a joke from *Without Feathers* where the Allen persona says, "Once again I tried committing suicide—this time by wetting my nose and inserting it into a light socket."[11]

When Sheldon first meets Treva, she, too, is presented as an expert on bathos. She asks Sheldon to wait a minute while she finishes a conversation she is having with a dead friend. She then continues by means of a small smoking bowl to give instructions to this friend on how to baste and cook a chicken.

Furthermore, Treva Marx has several traits in common with Sheldon's mother. Thus her very first remark to him when he comes to her for professional assistance is "Come in, Sheldon! You look terrible!" When he is upset, she immediately offers to boil him some chicken. Sheldon's reply, that his mother used to boil chicken and "render the bird devoid of any flavor," is again a repetition of a joke used in *Stardust Memories* where Sandy tells Dorrie that his mother used to run boiled chicken through a "deflavorizing machine." When Sadie finally decides that she can come down, it is because Treva says that her son "could use a little fattening, but otherwise he's a doll." These similarities between Sadie and Treva are reflected in Allen's choice of music. Thus the frivolous and irrepressible song which is played repeatedly throughout the film has the grossly Freudian title *I Want a Girl Just Like the Girl That Married Dear Old Dad!*

Sheldon eventually chooses the girl who most resembles his mother. Normally such a flagrant resignation toward an unresolved Oedipus complex would probably seem very despondent. (In fact, I recently had in one of my classes a woman who is a psychologist who felt that this short feature was extremely depressing.) In the context of the Allen universe, however, we realize that there are differences between Sadie and Treva which are ultimately more important than the similarities. When Sadie, primarily for the sake of Lisa's young children, is taken to the show, she gets totally unreasonable and keeps *kvetching*, "I'm not crazy about magic!" Like Enid Pollack, Paul's antimagic mother in *The Floating Lightbulb*, she has a stifling and destructive effect on her son. Like the mother about whom Isaac in *Manhattan* wrote a story, she is a classic example of the "Castrating Zionist."

Treva has the exact opposite effect on Sheldon. She is the one who represents magic and the capacity for hope. Sheldon tells her that he does not believe in her supernatural powers because "I'm a person who believes in science and logic and rational thought." With the unaffectedness of the *shlemiel* Treva answers: "Right, meanwhile your mother is hovering over the Chrysler Building!"

Although it seems as if all her invocations and incantations cannot bring Sadie down, Treva still insists: "I always had hopes. I always think that there's more to the world than meets the eye." Since Sadie is up there in the first place, she is right of course, and in the end it turns out to be the enchantment of Treva's personality that makes Sadie come down.

Despite the numerous sighs of relief that issued from various critics, "Oedipus Wrecks" is definitely one of Allen's more inessential and nugatory works. Its primary redeeming feature is the casting of the roles of Treva and Sadie. Julie Kavner was a strong presence in both *Hannah and Her Sisters* and *Radio Days* and is delightful as Treva, and Mae Questel is a perfect gem. In fact she ought to have been given an award for "Best Portrayal of a Jewish Mother Since Shelley Winters in *Next Stop Greenwich Village*." The scene where all hell breaks loose, accompanied by jungle drums on the sound track, as Sadie "invades" Sheldon's office together with the stone deaf Aunt Ceil and embarrasses him in front of his colleagues, is painfully recognizable and absolutely hilarious. The film finishes as it started with a close up of Sheldon who is now equivocally watching his mother and Treva discussing photos of him as a child.

For several years Allen has made frequent use of repetition and variations on his own themes. One often has the feeling which is expressed in the Harry James theme song from *Hannah and Her Sisters,* that one has "heard that song before." Usually, as in the song, this feeling is accompanied by a sense of nostalgia and the thrill of recognition.[12] In a few of Allen's films, such as "Oedipus Wrecks," these repetitions and variations seem stale and forced. In the second film which Allen released in 1989, however, they are once again used with exhilarating results.

In *September,* Stephanie told Peter that her husband was a radiologist: "He takes x-rays, but I never let him take them of me because if he looked inside, he'd see things that he wouldn't understand and he'd be terribly hurt." In the opening scene of *Another Woman,* Marion informed us that her husband was a "cardiologist who some years ago examined my heart, liked what he saw, and proposed." In *Crimes and Misdemeanors,* Woody Allen takes the use of a medical profession as a metaphor several steps further. Rather than being just mentioned in passing, the medical specialty of the main character of Allen's second 1989 project carries the central symbolic meaning of the film.

Like *Hannah and Her Sisters, Crimes and Misdemeanors* is an extremely complex film which tells several apparently unrelated stories, the connection between which we only see gradually. The central story is that of Judah Rosenthal, an immensely accomplished opthalmologist who finds his success marred by a frantic and unrelenting mistress who threatens to ruin both his career and his marriage if he leaves her. In the opening scene we witness a grand celebration of Judah's latest success. During his speech he says that although he is "a man of science" and "a skeptic," he feels that his prayers have been answered, and quotes his father who used to say that "the eyes of God are on us always." The party scene is intercut with a scene showing Judah at home before the celebration. He accidentally finds an unopened letter from Dolores, his mistress, addressed to his wife, Miriam. He opens it and reads a complete confession of their relationship. What we see during this scene is a beautifully composed close-up containing several elements involved in Judah's story: the threatening letter from Dolores in his hand, the wedding-band that he wears on that hand, his tightened gut, and a blazing fire in the background indicating infernal punishment. After reading Dolores's letter, he destroys it in that fire. Judah decides to ask his brother Jack, who is involved with the mob, to arrange to have Dolores neatly "removed." During the rest of the film, we witness Judah's struggle with his conscience.

Elegantly cross-edited with Judah's story is the secondary plot concerning Clifford Stern. Early in the film, Judah goes to Dolores's apartment to try and appease her, and while she is complaining about all the years she has wasted on their relationship, we cut to an old black-and-white movie of Carole Lombard venting the exact same feelings. The logical explanation for this cut is the fact that Clifford has taken his young niece, Jenny, to the Bleecker Street Cinema where they are watching Alfred Hitchcock's 1941 film *Mr. and Mrs. Smith.* Throughout, the film cross-cuts between what is happening to Judah and old movies that Clifford is watching which deal with the same themes.

Clifford is a filmmaker. He makes serious and noncommercial documentaries concerning such topics as "toxic waste" and "starving children," reflecting the fact that, like the Allen persona of the late 1970s, he is a socially and politically conscious moralist. Clifford is married to Wendy, but the two of them seem to have grown apart. When Wendy's brother Lester, who is a narcissistic television producer, asks Clifford to direct a TV biography of him, Clifford meets and falls in love with Halley Reed who is in charge of the series of biographies.

Again, as in Allen's earlier films, one can read the value and importance of any given relationship out of the things people do when they are together. Thus when Clifford comes home and tells Wendy that "a strange man defecated on my sister," and she continues reading *Commentary* unheedingly, we immediately, especially in the light of the relationship between Alvy Singer and his second wife, know that their marriage is over.

When Halley and Clifford are together, they do things that seem extremely nice. They play hooky to go to the movies in the afternoon, and spend evenings watching old films on Clifford's moviola while eating take-out food from an Indian restaurant. When we realize, however, that they keep talking through the lovely old films they are watching, we should be forewarned that the relationship is not going to last. Toward the end of the film Halley tells Clifford that, like Tracy in *Manhattan,* she is going to London to work. Like Ike, Clifford is devastated and tries to persuade her not to go. When we cut to the final scene, a wedding party, Halley and Clifford meet again several months later. It turns out, predictably enough, that unlike Tracy, Halley *has been* "corrupted," and she is now engaged to the superficial braggart Lester who proudly, and much to Clifford's consternation, tells everybody that "it was the caviar that did it."

In the final analysis, the one with whom Clifford, according to the Allen book of values, has the best time, is clearly his niece, Jenny. Jenny seems to be thoroughly enjoying the movies he takes her to see and the books he gives her. She listens attentively to his advice and precociously tries to help him solve his adult problems.

Whereas Wendy's brother Lester is pompous and "submental," her other brother, Ben, according to Clifford, is "a saint." Ben is a rabbi (played with great sweetness by Sam Waterston) who, in addition to being a wise and kind man, is also the link between the two main stories of the film, and the character who makes palpable the symbolism contained in Judah's profession.

Ben suffers from a serious eye disease and is a patient of Judah's. As Judah is going through hell trying to decide what to do about Dolores's threats, he asks for Ben's advice. Ben tells him that life and the universe are "harsh and empty of values" *unless* one acts according to "a moral structure with real meaning." When Judah decides to have Dolores killed, late at night alone in his living room he has a vision of Ben telling him that one is not allowed to take a human life. "You think," Ben admonishes Judah, "that God does not see?"

Repeatedly, eyes and the faculty of seeing are used figuratively. In a memory flash Judah sees himself and Dolores shortly after they have met. When she learns that he is an eye specialist, she asks him whether he believes that "they're the windows of the soul." When Jack calls to tell him that his orders have been carried out, Judah sees his father, Sol, who like Ben was a rabbi, telling him as a child that "the eyes of God see all" and that "the wicked will be punished for eternity." And when, almost against his will, Judah goes back to Dolores's apartment after she has been killed, he is stunned to find that there is "nothing behind her eyes" anymore, only a "black void."

Prompted by his guilt, Judah goes back to see his old house and is greeted by a scene from the past of a *Pesach Seder*. This ability to go back to the past and participate in it from one's present perspective we have seen in several of Allen's films, among them *Annie Hall* and most recently *Another Woman*. When presented with his son's dilemma and guilt, Judah's father, like Ben, talks about a "moral structure." Sol's radical sister, May, on the other hand is convinced that "if he chooses to ignore the ethics, he's home free." Sol, despite protests from his sister, tells the family that he would choose "God over truth" anytime, and he firmly believes that God will punish the wicked. "Sol's kind of faith is a gift," Judah's mother boasts.

In the last scene of the film, when the two main stories come together at the wedding of Ben's daughter, Julie, we learn that Ben's disease has turned out to be incurable, and he is now practically blind. Clifford and Wendy have split up, and, crushed by Halley's engagement to Lester and her lack of integrity, Clifford goes into an empty room to be alone. After a few minutes he is joined by Judah, whom he has never met before, and the two of them start talking. Knowing that Clifford is a filmmaker, Judah tells him the story of the murder, initially disguising it as an idea for a movie plot. We now learn that the man in Judah's story, who is of course himself, is as happy as ever. Eventually his sense of guilt has faded and things are "back to normal." Not only has he not been "punished" by God, but in fact he prospers. Clifford is horrified by the story and tries to convince the triumphant Judah that "in the absence of God, he has to assume responsibility himself." Judah brushes aside Clifford's philosophy with a cliché: "You're seeing too many movies—this is real life." (As usual in Allen's films, we are willing to accept the events of the movie as "real life.")

Reflected by the significant fact that Ben is irreversibly losing his eyesight, then, is the notion that God does *not* in fact see everything, presumably because the universe, as the Allen persona has claimed for years, is godless. The discordance between religion and politics that we find in Judah's family is a common enough phenomenon in twentieth-century Jewish American culture. The schism between Aunt May's belief in logic and rational thought and Sol's faith in God seems, furthermore, to reflect the typical Allenesque division of characters into those representing the brain and those representing the heart. We are told by Judah's daughter at the very end that her father "takes after May." It would appear that logic finally triumphs over faith in the Woody Allen film which concludes the decade of the 1980s. The usual element of magic is missing, and the faith of the *shlemiel* seems once again to be irrevocably undermined.

One would think, then, that *Crimes and Misdemeanors* is a bleak and dejected work. Certainly Woody Allen has expressed often enough lately that his view of life is gloomier than ever after the birth of his and Mia Farrow's baby. When the film is not depressing, but in fact uplifting, it is due to a subtle shift in the moral concerns of the persona.

As in *Another Woman,* we suddenly find characters that represent a balance between the heart and the brain. In addition to Ben, who is both intelligent and kindhearted, we are introduced to Dr. Louis Levy, an old Jewish "thinker" about whom Clifford would like to make a TV program for Halley's series. Clifford has a vast amount of footage of Dr. Levy philosophizing over the meaning of life, love, death, and the universe. Dr. Levy is equally capable of analyzing the theological implications of the Old Testament story of Abraham and Isaac, the coldness of the universe, and the functions of modern male/female relationships. Clifford even says that if he had known earlier what Levy has taught him about marriage, he could have avoided a gall bladder operation.

Toward the end of the film, Dr. Levy suddenly and unexpectedly commits suicide. He leaves behind only a note that says: "I've gone out the window." Clifford is very upset, partly because it ruins his plans to make a film, and partly because Levy "was a role model; you'd think he'd leave a decent note." Paradoxically, however, Levy's suicide does not seem as tragic as one would expect. One reason for this is that it has an eerie comparability to the suicide of Dr. Bruno Bettelheim, which took place five months after *Crimes and Misdemeanors* opened in the United States.[13] Bettelheim, who had a cameo role as one of the witnesses in *Zelig,* and who very much resembles Dr. Levy, had planned his suicide for over a year. He had decided that he could no longer live a dignified life and became a member of "The Hemlock Society."

On March 13, 1990, Bettelheim ended his life happily and peace-
fully, and all he left behind were four lines on a piece of paper in
his typewriter.

In an interview in February, a month before his death, Bettelheim talked about love and death as the two areas where
human beings have to make really significant choices. And Dr.
Levy in a voice-over ends the film with similar observations, on a
predominantly optimistic note. After Judah's confession to
Clifford, we see a collage repeating the happy moments of the
film, and finally Ben dancing with his newlywed daughter. On the
sound track we hear Louis Levy telling us that life consists of an
endless array of moral choices. "We define ourselves," he says, "by
the choices we have made." This is, of course, the epitome of the
existentialist ideas with which Allen has been toying at least since
Ike at the beginning of *Manhattan* asked the central question of
whether one of the characters would have the nerve to "dive into
the icy water" of the East River to save a stranger from drowning.
The same notion is the fundamental concern of Albert Camus's
book *The Fall,* one of the central works of the French Existentialist
movement of the 1950s, which Allen made fun of in "The Con-
demned" (one of the stories in *Side Effects*). Again, as in so many of
his films, Allen reminds us of the moral implications of the choices
made during the McCarthy era when he says of Lester: "I love
him like a brother. David Greenglass."[14]

The "crimes" of the title unequivocally refer to Judah's arranging to have Dolores murdered, whereas the "misdemeanors" are
more open to interpretation. Since Judah and Clifford finally
meet in the last scene (and are portrayed together on the poster
for the film), it is pertinent to assume that Clifford is the one who
is guilty of these misdemeanors. If we take Halley's word when she
tells him that Lester is not as bad as they thought, then Clifford's
bitterness toward and envy of Lester, who is rich and famous and
has managed to snare his love away from him with caviar, is an
unappealing, although perfectly understandable trait. It is possible, however, to take the opposite view that Halley is rationaliz-
ing to make excuses for her own choice. Certainly we never see
any indications that Lester is anything but an absolutely despica-
ble character.

In an interview in connection with the release of the film, Allen
commented on this aspect, describing it as a "problem that I think
exists all over the United States, and that is this tremendous
worship of success so that when someone is successful, everyone,
from the average person to even intellectuals, will rationalize the

positive quality of their work, whether it has any merit or not." He continues to say that "I think those people who are undeserving successes know the real truth when they go to bed at night. So I do think Alan Alda [i.e., Lester] is aware that he is not as good as everyone tells him."[15] On the basis of Allen's own view of the film, then, Lester is guilty of the "misdemeanor" of knowingly being an "undeserving success." But more importantly, Hadley, who is intelligent and, according to the Allen book of moral codes, ought to know better, is guilty of the "misdemeanor" of worshipping Lester's success and consequently not acting according to her convictions. Her choice, in existentialist terms, is inauthentic.

According to the film, then, it is ultimately our own individual responsibility whether or not we choose to commit these crimes and misdemeanors. There may be no almighty and all-seeing God to punish us, but that does not mean that we are free to do as we please. In the absence of God, as Clifford says, we have to assume responsibility ourselves. The only thing which gives any meaning to the universe that the Allen persona has been so worried about, is precisely, Ben says to Judah, our acting according to "a moral structure." And we are, as Levy says, "the sum total of our choices."

Despite its anticlimactic ending, *Crimes and Misdemeanors* contains an undeniable optimism. This is reflected in the fact that the film, although it takes place in the fall, indicating decay, is suffused with a radiant, golden light that has a very soothing and invigorating effect. Furthermore, Dr. Levy goes on to tell us that although "the universe is a pretty cold place" where "human happiness does not seem to be included," it is our "capacity to love" that finally makes it all worthwhile. He ends the film—while Ben is dancing with Julie—by saying that we all have to "hope that future generations might understand more."

The idea that love is the only hope in a disconsolate and cruel universe is by no means new in Allen's work. In fact, it has been the central solution to the worries and obsessions of his persona from the very beginning. What is relatively new is the concern with coming generations. It is significant that the celebration at the end of the film is a wedding. And the fact that Jenny is the one with whom Clifford has the best time is important. Thus it is no coincidence that Clifford is with her when he gets the message from his answering service of Dr. Levy's death. (The only message he ever does get.) He has just been confiding in her that in matters of love, it is very hard getting one's head and one's heart to agree: "In my case they're not even friendly."

We saw earlier how Mia Farrow's entering Allen's life and works helped solve the basic conflicts of the persona. Now, as Allen has entered his fifties, he and Farrow have adopted a little girl, Dylan, who has already had cameo roles in Allen's films (as Joe's sister in *Radio Days* and as Lisa's youngest child in *New York Stories*) and recently Farrow gave birth to Allen's first child. His own opinion on how this has affected him is that "it has made me more depressed." The reason for this, Allen says, is that:

> I have these two babies, really, this girl and this boy. And I look at them—they're so cute and so innocent and so sweet—and I think "They don't know how terrible the world is," you know, . . . and they have got to fight off a million diseases and heartbreaks and ignorant people and warring countries and they're just two sweet kids.[16]

Despite Allen's pessimism, however, the notion of parenthood (especially motherhood) and the concern with posterity have been absolutely central in all his works in the last half of the 1980s. *September* and "Oedipus Wrecks"—the least interesting works of the period—portray the devastating effects of the mother, and both are seen from the point of view of the child. *Another Woman* is a much more nuanced work at the center of which we find concepts such as pregnancy and childbearing as opposed to abortion. Its central character is allowed at the end to represent a newfound balance, so that the emotional and the intellectual are no longer portrayed as dichotomous and thus mutually exclusive, but are amalgamated into a synthesis. At the end of *Hannah and Her Sisters,* Holly informs Mickey that she is pregnant, and the Allen persona thus assumes the role of parent rather than child. Both *Radio Days* and *Crimes and Misdemeanors* end with hopeful speculations about future generations.

In Anne Tyler's wonderful novel *The Accidental Tourist* the central character, Macon Leary, reluctantly has to admit that he is able to feel love and responsibility for the son of Muriel Pritchett after the tragic death of his own son Ethan. He feels "a pleasant kind of sorrow sweeping through him. Oh, his life had regained all its old perils. He was forced to worry once again about nuclear war and the future of the planet. He often had the same secret guilty thought that had come to him after Ethan was born: *From this time on I can never be completely happy.* Not that he was before, of course."[17] In Allen's films of the late 1980s, the main function of these heirs and aftercomers is likewise to put into perspective our own lives so that we understand the importance of the choices we have to make.

In one of the last scenes of *Hannah and Her Sisters,* the Allen persona goes into the movie theater to get himself together after his abortive suicide attempt. Looking at the Marx Brothers up on the screen, he realizes that he has to give up trying to find all the answers about the hostile and potentially godless universe, and instead try to "enjoy it while it lasts." The implication is that the answers to his questions are to be found in this life. Strangely enough, the solution that Mickey reaches sounds very much like the advice that young Alvy Singer got from Doctor Flicker when he was worried about his newfound knowledge that the universe is expanding. "It won't be expanding for billions of years yet," Doctor Flicker told him. "And we've gotta try to enjoy ourselves while we're here. Uh?"

Finally, what *Crimes and Misdemeanors* adds to the knowledge that the Allen persona has attained over the past decades is the notion that life and the universe are only "harsh and empty of values" if we do not act according to "a moral structure." It may very well turn out that we "only go around once" and that the universe is cruel and meaningless. It may be possible to commit atrocious crimes and various misdemeanors without being punished by an all-seeing God. But that does not absolve us from being responsible for our own actions.

When Marion of *Another Woman* goes through her mother's things, she finds a poem by Rainer Maria Rilke which says that: "Here there is no place that does not see you. You must change your life!" Just as the existentialist theories of Jean-Paul Sartre had been moved out of Kirkegaard's realm of theology and into that of ethics and politics, so the notion which is at the center of this poem is not a religious notion of the eyes of God which see all, but an ethical one. Thus, if there "is no place" that does not see us, and if human beings are the "sum total" of their choices, then it is finally up to the Allen persona himself, by means of his moral choices, to put meaning into his own everyday life in New York City, and in effect into the empty universe.

In conclusion it would seem that the Allen persona has finally found an answer to the obsessions which have haunted him ever since Alvy Singer was unable to do his homework because he had read that "the universe is expanding!" I guess that one might argue that whereas it is entirely possible that the universe is in fact expanding, ultimately it would seem that it is up to each and every one of us to prove that it is equally possible that Alvy Singer's mother was right when she flagrantly proclaimed that "Brooklyn is not expanding!"

Notes

All quotations from the stand-up routines are taken from *The Nightclub Years, 1964–1968*, United Artists. UA 9968, 1976.

Preface

1. *To Woody Allen from Europe with Love.*

Chapter 1: A Shlemiel Is Born (1960–1969)

1. Howe, *World of Our Fathers*, 545.
2. A detailed and entertaining, although possibly not completely factual description of the Allen/Rosen marriage can be found in McKnight.
3. Edwin Miller, "The Tallest Dwarf in the World," *Seventeen Interviews: Filmstars and Superstars*, 237.
4. Lax, *Woody Allen and His Comedy*, 40.
5. This makes Harlene Rosen's lawsuits for defamation of character (1967–1969) seem more than slightly humorless.
6. Leo Rosten argues that the word *shlemiel* should be spelled with only the "sh" because "in English to begin a word with 'sch' is to call for a 'sk' sound" (Rosten 352). I have thus chosen to spell *shlemiel* with "sch" only when I quote from other works.
7. Wisse, *The Schlemiel as Modern Hero*, 14.
8. Ibid., x.
9. Herman, comp., *The Book of Hollywood Quotes*, 96.
10. Rosenblum and Karen, *When the Shooting Stops*, 264.
11. Quite a few of these can be found in Guthrie.
12. Rosenblum and Karen, *When the Shooting Stops*, 264.
13. Henri Bergson, "Laughter," *Comedy*, Wylie Sypher, ed., 113.
14. Cohen, ed., *The Essential Lenny Bruce*, 5.
15. Quote taken from Bob Fosse's film *All That Jazz*.
16. Guthrie, *Woody Allen*, 101.
17. Lax, *Woody Allen and His Comedy*, 98–99.
18. Adler and Feinman, *Woody Allen. Clown Prince*, 19.
19. For an extensive analysis that does more than justice to the film, see Yacowar, *Loser Take All*, 26–35.
20. It should be noted that the problem with the film is not its theme as such. Warren Beatty, who was originally cast as Michael James, proved with his 1975 movie *Shampoo* that when treated with delicacy and insight, the compulsive Don Juan theme can be both funny and moving.
21. Yacowar, *Loser Take All*, 35.
22. Jacobs, *. . . but we need*, 35–36.

23. I am indebted to Maurice Yacowar without whose detailed analysis of the film my own would not have been possible as it was never shown in Denmark.

24. Jacobs, . . . *but we need*, 5.

25. In his analysis, Yacowar also divides the Allen persona into three, but with rather a different emphasis. I disagree with his theory that Walter Hollander is a middle-class "insider" who is forced into the position of the "outsider" and thus made aware of his own fragility. His complaints about his hernia and other defects are not newly acquired traits but part of his being a classic *kvetch*. Walter is not made aware of *anything*. He disrupts the embassy, not the other way around.

26. Guthrie, *Woody Allen*, 55.

27. Edwin Miller, "The Tallest Dwarf in the World," *Seventeen Interviews: Filmstars and Superstars*, 244.

28. The Hollanders's daughter, Susan, (one of the minor characters) is often called "the embodiment of common sense," or the voice of reason in the play (Jacobs 30). But although she seems calmer and less frantic than her parents, she is no more realistic. She does not understand the gravity of this abnormal situation either, but finds the whole experience "exciting and romantic." Accordingly, rather than trying to cope, she falls in love.

Chapter 2: Here's Looking at You, Kid! (1969–1971)

1. Cervantes, *Don Quixote*, 32.

2. Quoted in Jacobs, . . . *but we need*, 17.

3. Henri Bergson, "Laughter," in *Comedy* Wylie Sypher, ed., 69.

4. Herman, comp., *The Book of Hollywood Quotes*, 85.

5. The epitome of the comic who inspires harsh laughter because of the audience's identification with his dreams, visions, and nightmares is, of course, Lenny Bruce.

6. Dooley, *From Scarface to Scarlett*, 295.

7. Warshow, *The Immediate Experience*, 133.

8. Allen, *Getting Even*, 16.

9. Ibid., 95.

10. Perelman, *The Most of S. J. Perelman*, 369.

11. Allen, *Getting Even*, 40.

12. Ibid., 37.

13. Ibid., 25.

14. Ibid., 89–90.

15. Probst, *Off Camera*, 259.

16. Jacobs, . . . *but we need*, 71.

Chapter 3: Among the Very Young at Heart? (1971–1976)

1. Hellman, *Scoundrel Time*, 98.

2. The title *Bananas* refers partly to the fact that San Marcos is a banana republic, partly to the expression to "go bananas," and perhaps it is also a homage to the Marx Brothers, one of whose films was called *Coconuts*.

3. Lasch, *The Culture of Narcissism*, 51.

4. A further irony arises when one keeps in mind that in the essay "Viva Vargas!" in *Getting Even*, the rebel leader was called Vargas. In *Bananas*, the ruthless dictator is.

5. In an essay in *Without Feathers,* Allen claims that the Russian Revolution "erupted when the serfs finally realized that the Czar and the Tsar was the same person." (Allen, *Without Feathers,* 107).

6. Lax, *Woody Allen and His Comedy,* 66.

7. Chaplin, *My Autobiography,* 506.

8. Wolf, *Landmark Films,* 384–85.

9. Probst, *Off Camera,* 261.

10. Wisse, *The Schlemiel as Modern Hero,* 6.

11. Lax, *Woody Allen and His Comedy,* 227.

12. Tolstoy, *Anna Karenina,* 823.

13. Jack Kroll, "Funny, but He's Serious," *Newsweek,* April 24, 1978, 49.

14. Lax, *Woody Allen and His Comedy,* 104.

15. Ibid., 45.

16. Tolstoy, *Anna Karenina,* 812–13.

17. Allen, *Without Feathers,* 5.

18. Ibid., 25.

19. Ibid., 23–24.

20. Ibid., 5–6.

21. Ibid., 102.

22. Ibid., 60–61.

23. Ibid., 72.

24. Guthrie, *Woody Allen,* 154.

25. Ibid., 157.

26. Probably Howard's cowardice is related to the dread of poverty so characteristic of people who came of age during the depression, and which Allen described in his parents. For the first time in his life, Howard can afford a proper apartment. Becoming involved in Florence's cause would inevitably entail having to give up the security he has finally found.

27. Hellman, *Scoundrel Time,* 53.

28. Ibid., 86.

29. Ibid., 98.

Chapter 4: A Little Faith in People (1977–1979)

1. George and Ira Gershwin, *But Not for Me,* in Ira Gershwin, *Lyrics on Several Occasions,* 234.

2. In *Manhattan,* the Allen persona writes a story about his mother called "The Castrating Zionist."

3. Lasch, *The Culture of Narcissism,* 33, 37, and 50.

4. Ibid., 177.

5. It is interesting to note that Allen chose nonactor Paul Simon to play the part of Alvy's rival. Possibly the reason for this is that Simon is about the only person he could find who is shorter than he is.

6. In a number of Allen's films made after *The Front,* we see elements of the main concern of that film. The Allen persona becomes increasingly obsessed, if not so much with the actual hearings, then at least with the *idea* of the McCarthyist era, of betraying and informing on one's friends. In *Manhattan,* the persona accuses his friend, Yale, of being ready to inform on him should the occasion ever arise. And in an early version of *Annie Hall,* which was originally entitled *Anhedonia,* there was a nightmare scene in which Alvy was tortured by

Nazis but refused to give them the names of his associates. Like the early Allen persona, however, he is a coward. He pulls a hand puppet from his pocket and says, "Because of my moral convictions, I cannot name names. But *he* (indicating the puppet) can."

7. "Love, Death and La-De-Dah," *Time*, September 26, 1977, 43.

8. Lax, *Woody Allen and His Comedy*, 124.

9. Ibid., 72.

10. Vernon Young, "Autumn Interiors," *Commentary*, January 1979, 61.

11. Palmer, *Woody Allen*, 47.

12. Monaco, *American Film Now*, 245.

13. Lax, *Woody Allen and His Comedy*, 172.

14. The part of Jill is played by a twenty-six-year-old Meryl Streep who, seven years and a world of fame later, was to portray a real-life counterpart to Jill in the Mike Nichols film *Heartburn*, based on Nora Ephron's script.

15. Wisse, *The Schlemiel as Modern Hero*, 91.

Chapter 5: Stardust (1980–1982)

1. Pells, *The Liberal Mind*, 1.

2. Quoted in Becker, *The Denial of Death*, 199.

3. Allen, *Side Effects*, 75.

4. Ibid., 74.

5. Becker, *The Denial of Death*, 159.

6. Ibid., 168.

7. Allen, *Side Effects*, 136.

8. Ibid., 145.

9. Ibid., 149.

10. In certain ways Isobel resembles Mia Farrow, and one cannot help but wonder whether this incident is in any way based on Woody Allen's first meeting with *her* children.

11. Monaco, 245.

12. Gene Siskel, "Woody Allen on Love, Films, and Reagan," *Chicago Tribune*, July 11, 1982.

Chapter 6: Isn't It Romantic? (1983–1986)

1. Boorstin, *The Image*, 6.

2. Howe, *World of Our Fathers*, 68.

3. Boorstin, *The Image*, 57.

4. Ibid., 46–48.

5. Ibid., 70.

6. Schickel, *Intimate Strangers*, 3.

7. Boorstin, *The Image*, 73.

8. Possibly Allen is also making fun of Warren Beatty's witnesses in *Reds*, which Beatty made after Diane Keaton and Allen had split up, and Keaton had moved in with Beatty.

9. Levine, *E. L. Doctorow*, 59.

10. In fact, in many ways *Zelig* is truer to the idea of Doctorow's novel than Milos Forman's adaptation is.

11. Schickel, *Intimate Strangers*, 17.

12. Boorstin, *The Image*, 46.

13. Andrew Sarris, "Woody Allen at the Peak of Parody," *Village Voice*, July 10, 1983.

14. Boorstin, *The Image*, 6.

15. Quoted in Howe, *World of Our Fathers*, 637.

16. It should be noted here that Mia Farrow's acting in this part is absolutely astounding. Her portrayal of the hard-boiled Tina is so convincing and so different from the fragile, elfin characters that Farrow used to play that it takes a while before you even recognize her.

17. For further information see chapter 5.

18. Wolf, *Landmark Films*, 384.

19. Kael, *State of the Art*, 339.

20. Nick Rosen, "Hurricane Woody Hits Town" [sic], *Sunday Times*, London, May 6, 1984.

21. Kael, *State of the Art*, 26–27.

Chapter 7: I've Heard That Song Before (1987–1989)

1. The closing lines from Woody Allen's *Another Woman*.

2. Richard Corliss, "Retro-Romance in a Swanky Town," *Time*, February 3, 1986, 43.

3. Some of the children are Mia Farrow's own.

4. Cf. the ending of *Sleeper* in chapter 3.

5. Navacelle, *Woody Allen on Location*, 216.

6. Ibid., 463.

7. This and all the other songs are played by Bernie Leighton whom Allen also uses in "Oedipus Wrecks," and who actually has a cameo appearance in *Another Woman* as a party pianist.

8. Fitzgerald, *The Great Gatsby*, 186.

9. Mia Farrow, who is Lane, played Daisy, of course, but one does not really think about that because in this film she looks a lot more like Liv Ullmann than like Daisy Buchanan.

10. Jack Kroll, "Funny, but He's Serious," *Newsweek*, April 24, 1978, 49.

11. Allen, *Without Feathers*, 4.

12. In fact, while Allen was going through his most recent experimental phase of "serious" films like *September* and *Another Woman*, Rob Reiner managed to cash in on the popular yearning for bittersweet Allen films in the style of *Annie Hall* with his delightful, semi-autobiographical *When Harry Met Sally*.

13. It should be mentioned that *Crimes and Misdemeanors* opened in Denmark several months after its American opening, and after Bettelheim's death. I thus had the benefit of a false retrospect when I first saw the film.

14. David Greenglass was the brother of Ethel Rosenberg whose testimony sent the Rosenbergs to the electric chair.

15. Silvio Bizio, "The Importance of Being Woody," *Empire*, August 1990, 48.

16. Ibid., 50.

17. Tyler, *The Accidental Tourist*, 257–58.

Filmography

Primary Sources

The Woody Allen Filmography

What's New, Pussycat? (1965)
Director, Clive Donner. Producer: Charles Feldman. Screenplay: Woody Allen. Photography: Jean Badal. Music: Burt Bacharach. Editor: Fergus McDonell. A Famous Artists production. 120 minutes. Peter Sellers (Fritz Fassbender). Peter O'Toole (Michael James). Romy Schneider (Carol Werner). Capucine (Renée Lefebvre). Paula Prentiss (Liz Bien). Woody Allen (Victor Shakapopolis). Ursula Andress (Rita).

What's Up, Tiger Lily? (1966)
Original version: *Kagi No Kagi* (Key of Keys), (Japan, 1964). Director: Senkichi Taniguchi. Script: Hideo Ando. Photography: Kazuo Yamada. Produced by Tomoyuki Tanaka for Toho. 94 minutes. Re-release Director: Woody Allen. Production Conception: Ben Shapiro. Editor: Richard Krown. Script and Dubbing: Woody Allen, Frank Buxton, Len Maxwell, Louise Lasser, Mickey Rose, Julie Bennett, Bryna Wilson. Music: The Lovin' Spoonful. 79 minutes. Tatsuya Mihashi (Phil Moskowitz). Mie Hana (Terry Yaki). Akiko Wakayabayashi (Suki Yaki). Tadao Nakamaru (Shepherd Wong). Susumu Kurobe (Wing Fat).

Casino Royale (1967)
Directors: John Huston, Kenneth Hughes, Val Guest, Robert Parrish, Joseph McGrath. Producers: Charles Feldman and Jerry Bresler. Screenplay: Wolf Mankowitz, John Law, Michael Sayers, suggested by the novel by Ian Fleming. Photography: Jack Hildyard. Editor: Bill Lenny. Music: Burt Bacharach. A Famous Artists Production, released by Columbia Pictures. 131 minutes. Peter Sellers (Evelyn Tremble). Ursula Andress (Vesper Lynd). David Niven (Sir James Bond). Orson Welles (Le Chiffre). Joanna Pettet (Mata Bond). Deborah Kerr (Widow McTarry). Daliah Lavi (The Detainer). Woody Allen (Jimmy Bond). William Holden (Ransome). Charles Boyer (Le Grand). John Huston (M). George Raft (Himself).

Don't Drink the Water! (1969)
Director: Howard Morris. Producer: Charles Joffe. Screenplay: R. S. Allen and Harvey Bullock. Based upon the stageplay by Woody Allen. Photography: Harvey Genkins. Editor: Ralph Rosenblum. 98 minutes. Jackie Gleason (Walter Hollander). Estelle Parsons (Marion Hollander). Ted Bessell (Axel Magee). Joan Delaney (Susan Hollander). Richard Libertini (Father Drobney). Michael Constantine (Krojack). Avery Schreiber (Sultan).

149

Take the Money and Run! (1969)
Director: Woody Allen. Script: Woody Allen and Mickey Rose. Photography: Lester Shorr. Editing: Paul Jordan, Ron Kalish. Music: Marvin Hamlisch. Art Director: Fred Harpman. Special Effects: A. D. Flowers. Assistant Directors: Louis Stroller, Walter Hill. Produced by Charles H. Joffe for Palomar Pictures. 85 minutes. Woody Allen (Virgil Starkwell). Janet Margolin (Louise). Marcel Hillaire (Fritz). Jacqueline Hyde (Miss Blair). Lonnie Chapman (Jake). Jan Merlin (Al). James Anderson (Chain gang warden). Howard Storm (Red). Ethel Sokolow (Virgil's mother). Henry Leff (Virgil's father). Don Frazier (Psychiatrist). Louise Lasser (Kay Lewis). Jackson Beck (Narrator).

Bananas (1971)
Director: Woody Allen. Script: Woody Allen and Mickey Rose. Photography: Andrew M. Costikyan. Music: Marvin Hamlisch. Editor: Ron Kalish. Associate Producer: Ralph Rosenblum. Assistant Director: Fred T. Gallo. Produced by Jack Grossberg. A Jack Rollins-Charles H. Joffe Production. 81 minutes. Woody Allen (Fielding Mellish). Louise Lasser (Nancy). Carlos Montalban (General Vargas). Natividad Abascal (Yolanda). Jacobo Morales (Esposito). Howard Cosell (Himself). Roger Grimsby (Himself). Don Dunphy (Himself). Charlotte Rae (Mrs. Mellish). Stanley Ackerman (Dr. Mellish).

Play It Again, Sam! (1972)
Director: Herbert Ross. Production Supervisor: Roger M. Rothstein. Screenplay: Woody Allen, based on his stageplay. Photography: Owen Roizman. Music: Billy Goldenberg. Editor: Marion Rothman. Assistant Director: William Gerrity. An Arthur P. Jacobs Production for Paramount Pictures. 84 minutes. Woody Allen (Allan Felix). Diane Keaton (Linda Christie). Tony Roberts (Dick Christie). Jerry Lacy (Humphrey Bogart). Susan Anspach (Nancy). Jennifer Salt (Sharon). Joy Bang (Julie). Viva (Jennifer). Suzanne Zenor (Discotheque girl). Diana Davila (Museum girl). Mari Fletcher (Fantasy Sharon). Michael Green and Ted Markland (Hoods).

Everything You Always Wanted to Know About Sex (*but were afraid to ask) (1972)
Director: Woody Allen. Script: Woody Allen, from the book by David Reuben. Photography: David M. Walsh. Assistant Directors: Fred T. Gallo, Terry M. Carr. Editor: Eric Albertson. Produced by Charles H. Joffe for United Artists. 87 minutes. Woody Allen (Fool, Fabrizio, Victor Shakapopolis, Sperm). John Carradine (Dr. Bernardo). Lou Jacobi (Sam). Louise Lasser (Gina). Anthony Quayle (King). Tony Randall (Operator). Lynn Redgrave (Queen). Burt Reynolds (Switchboard). Gene Wilder (Dr. Ross). Jack Barry (Himself). Heather Macrae (Helen). Baruch Lumet (Rabbi Baumel). Robert Walden (Sperm).

Sleeper (1973)
Director: Woody Allen. Script: Woody Allen, Marshall Brickman. Photography: David M. Walsh. Editor: Ralph Rosenblum. Production Designer: Dale Hennesy. Assistant Directors: Fred T. Gallo, Henry J. Lange, Jr. Special Effects: A. D. Flowers. Music by Woody Allen with the Preservation Hall Jazz Band and the New Orleans Funeral Ragtime Orchestra. Produced by Jack Grossberg. A Jack Rollins-Charles H. Joffe Production. 88 minutes. Woody Allen (Miles Monroe). Diane Keaton (Luna Schlosser). John Beck (Erno Windt).

Love and Death (1975)

Director: Woody Allen. Script: Woody Allen. Photography: Ghislain Cloquet. Editors: Ralph Rosenblum, Ron Kalish. Assistant Directors: Paul Feyder, Bernard Cohn. Music: Sergei Prokofiev. Costume Designer: Gladys De Segonzac. Produced by Charles H. Joffe. A Jack Rollins-Charles H. Joffe Production. 85 minutes. Woody Allen (Boris). Diane Keaton (Sonia). Georges Adet (Old Nehamken). Lloyd Battista (Don Francisco). Henry Czarniak (Ivan). Despo Diamantidou (Mother). Olga Georges-Picot (Countess Alexandrovna). Harold Gould (Count Anton). Jessica Harper (Natasha). Alfred Lutter III (Young Boris). James Tolkan (Napoleon).

The Front (1976)

Produced and Directed by Martin Ritt. Script: Walter Bernstein. Music: Dave Grusin. Photography: Michael Chapman. Editor: Sidney Levin. Assistant Directors: Peter Scoppa, Ralph Singleton. A Martin Ritt-Jack Rollins-Charles H. Joffe Production. Distributed by Columbia Pictures. 94 minutes. Woody Allen (Howard Prince). Zero Mostel (Hecky Brown). Herschel Bernardi (Phil Sussman). Michael Murphy (Alfred Miller). Andrea Marcovicci (Florence Barrett). Remak Ramsay (Hennessey).

Annie Hall (1977)

Director: Woody Allen. Script: Woody Allen and Marshall Brickman. Photography: Gordon Willis. Editor: Ralph Rosenblum. Art Director: Mel Bourne. Animated Sequences: Chris Ishii. Assistant Directors: Fred T. Gallo, Fred Blankfein. Costume Designer: Ruth Morley. Produced by Charles H. Joffe. A Jack Rollins-Charles H. Joffe Production. Distributed by United Artists. 93 minutes. Woody Allen (Alvy Singer). Diane Keaton (Annie Hall). Tony Roberts (Rob). Carol Kane (Allison Porchnik). Paul Simon (Tony Lacey). Shelley Duvall (Rolling Stone Reporter, Pam). Janet Margolin (Robin). Colleen Dewhurst (Mom Hall). Christopher Walken (Duane). Donald Symington (Dad Hall). Helen Ludlam (Grammy Hall). Mordecai Lawner (Mr. Singer). Joan Newman (Mrs. Singer). Jonathan Munk (Alvy aged nine). Hy Ansel (Joey Nichols). Rashel Novikoff (Aunt Tessie). Russell Horton (Man in theater line). Marshall McLuhan (Himself). Dick Cavett (Himself). Robin Mary Paris (Actress in rehearsal). Charles Levin (Actor in rehearsal).

Interiors (1978)

Written and Directed by Woody Allen. Photography: Gordon Willis. Editor: Ralph Rosenblum. Production Designer: Mel Bourne. Assistant Director: Martin Berman. Costume Designer: Joel Schumacher. Produced by Charles H. Joffe. A Jack Rollins-Charles H. Joffe Production. Distributed by United Artists. 93 minutes. Kristen Griffith (Flynn). Marybeth Hurt (Joey). Richard Jordan (Frederick). Diane Keaton (Renata). E. G. Marshall (Arthur). Geraldine Page (Eve). Maureen Stapleton (Pearl). Sam Waterston (Mike).

Manhattan (1979)

Director: Woody Allen. Script: Woody Allen and Marshall Brickman. Photography: Gordon Willis. Editor: Susan E. Morse. Production Designer: Mel Bourne. Costumes: Albert Wolsky. Music: George Gershwin. Assistant Directors: Fredric B. Blankfein, Joan Spiegel Feinstein. Executive Producer: Robert Greenhut. Produced by Charles H. Joffe. A Jack Rollins-Charles H. Joffe Production.

152   BROOKLYN IS NOT EXPANDING

Distributed by United Artists. 96 minutes. Woody Allen (Isaac Davis). Diane Keaton (Mary Wilke). Michael Murphy (Yale). Mariel Hemingway (Tracy). Meryl Streep (Jill). Anne Byrne (Emily). Bella Abzug (Herself). Damion Sheller (Willie). Wallace Shawn (Jeremiah).

Stardust Memories (1980)
Written and Directed by Woody Allen. Photography: Gordon Willis. Editor: Susan E. Morse. Production Designer: Mel Bourne. Costumes: Santo Loquasto. Assistant Director: Fredric B. Blankfein. Executive Producers: Jack Rollins and Charles H. Joffe. Produced by Robert Greenhut. A Jack Rollins-Charles H. Joffe Production. Distributed by United Artists. 89 minutes. Woody Allen (Sandy Bates). Charlotte Rampling (Dorrie). Jessica Harper (Daisy). Marie-Christine Barrault (Isobel). Tony Roberts (Tony Roberts). Amy Wright (Shelley). Helen Hanft (Vivian Orkin). Anne De Salvo (Sandy's sister). Joan Neuman (Sandy's mother). Ken Chapin (Sandy's father). Eli Mintz (Old man). Robert Munk (Sandy as a child). Sharon Stone (Pretty girl on train).

A Midsummer Night's Sex Comedy (1982)
Written and Directed by Woody Allen. Photography: Gordon Willis. Editor: Susan E. Morse. Production Designer: Mel Bourne. Assistant Directors: Fredric B. Blankfein, Thomas Reilly, Anthony Gittelson. Executive Producer: Charles H. Joffe. Music: Felix Mendelsohn. Produced by Robert Greenhut. A Jack Rollins-Charles H. Joffe Production. Distributed by Orion Pictures and Warner Bros. Woody Allen (Andrew). Mia Farrow (Ariel). Tony Roberts (Maxwell). Jose Ferrer (Leopold). Julie Hagerthy (Dulcy). Mary Steenburgen (Adrian).

Zelig (1983)
Written and Directed by Woody Allen. Photography: Gordon Willis. Editor: Susan E. Morse. Costume Designer: Santo Loquasto. Production Designer: Mel Bourne. Executive Producer: Charles H. Joffe. Produced by Robert Greenhut. A Jack Rollins-Charles H. Joffe Production. Released by Orion Pictures and Warner Bros. 84 minutes. Woody Allen (Leonard Zelig). Mia Farrow (Dr. Eudora Fletcher). Susan Sontag, Irving Howe, Saul Bellow, Bricktop, Dr. Bruno Bettelheim, John Morton Blum (Themselves). Ed Herlihy, Dwight Weist, Gordon Gould, Windy Craig, Jurgen Kuehn (Announcers).

Broadway Danny Rose (1984)
Written and Directed by Woody Allen. Photography: Gordon Willis. Editor: Susan E. Morse. Costume Designer: Jeffrey Kurland. Production Designer: Mel Bourne. Executive Producer: Charles H. Joffe. Produced by Robert Greenhut. A Jack Rollins-Charles H. Joffe Production. Released by Orion Pictures. 85 minutes. Woody Allen (Danny Rose), Mia Farrow (Tina Vitale), Nick Apollo Forte (Lou Canova), Corbett Monica (Himself), Howard Storm (Himself), Morty Gunty (Himself), Will Jordan (Himself), Jackie Gayle (Himself), Jack Rollins (Himself), Sandy Baron (Himself), Milton Berle (Himself), Howard Cosell (Himself), Herb Reynold (Barney Dunn), Sandy Richman (Teresa), Olga Barbato (Angelina).

The Purple Rose of Cairo (1985)
Written and Directed by Woody Allen. Photography: Gordon Willis. Editor: Susan E. Morse. Costume Designer: Jeffrey Kurland. Production Designer:

Stuart Wurtzel. Executive Producer: Charles H. Joffe. Produced by Robert Greenhut. A Jack Rollins-Charles H. Joffe Production. Released by Orion Pictures. 82 minutes. Mia Farrow (Cecilia), Jeff Daniels (Tom Baxter/Gil Shepherd), Danny Aiello (Monk), Stephanie Farrow (Cecilia's sister), Dianne Wiest (Emma).

Hannah and Her Sisters (1986)
Written and Directed by Woody Allen. Photography: Carlo Di Palma. Editor: Susan E. Morse. Costume Designer: Jeffrey Kurland. Production Designer: Stuart Wurtzel, Woody Allen. Executive Producers: Jack Rollins, Charles H. Joffe. Produced by Robert Greenhut. A Jack Rollins-Charles H. Joffe Production. Released by Orion Pictures. 107 minutes. Mia Farrow (Hannah), Barbara Hershey (Lee), Dianne Wiest (Holly), Michael Caine (Elliot), Max Von Sydow (Frederick), Woody Allen (Mickey), Carrie Fisher (April), Maureen O'Sullivan (Norma), Lloyd Nolan (Evan), Julie Kavner (Gail), Daniel Stern (Dusty), Daisy Previn, Moses Farrow, Allen Decheser, Artie Decheser (Hannah's children), Ivan Kronenfeld (Lee's husband).

Radio Days (1987)
Written and Directed by Woody Allen. Photography: Carlo Di Palma. Editor: Susan E. Morse. Costume Designer: Jeffrey Kurland. Production Designer: Santo Loquasto. Executive Producers: Jack Rollins, Charles H. Joffe. Produced by Robert Greenhut. A Jack Rollins-Charles H. Joffe Production. Released by Orion Pictures. 85 minutes. Mia Farrow (Sally White), Seth Green (Joe), Julie Kavner (Joe's mother), Dianne Wiest (Bea), Josh Mostel (Abe), Michael Tucker (Joe's father), Diane Keaton (Monica Charles, a nightclub singer), Wallace Shawn (The Masked Avenger), Jeff Daniels (Biff Baxter), Tony Roberts ("Silver Dollar Jackpot" Emcee).

September (1987)
Written and Directed by Woody Allen. Photography: Carlo Di Palma. Editor: Susan E. Morse. Costume Designer: Jeffrey Kurland. Production Designer: Santo Loquasto. Executive Producers: Jack Rollins, Charles H. Joffe. Produced by Robert Greenhut. A Jack Rollins-Charles H. Joffe Production. Released by Orion Pictures. 82 minutes. Denholm Elliott (Howard), Dianne Wiest (Stephanie), Mia Farrow (Lane), Elaine Stritch (Diane), Sam Waterston (Peter), Jack Warden (Lloyd).

Another Woman (1988)
Written and Directed by Woody Allen. Photography: Sven Nykvist. Editor: Susan E. Morse. Costume Designer: Jeffrey Kurland. Production Designer: Santo Loquasto. Executive Producers: Jack Rollins, Charles H. Joffe. Produced by Robert Greenhut. A Jack Rollins-Charles H. Joffe Production. Released by Orion Pictures. 81 minutes. Gena Rowlands (Marion), Mia Farrow (Hope), Ian Holm (Ken), Blythe Danner (Lydia), Bruce Jay Friedman (Mark), Gene Hackman (Larry), Betty Buckley (Kathy), Martha Plimpton (Laura), John Houseman (Marion's father), Sandy Dennis (Claire), Harris Yullin (Paul), Frances Conroy (Lynn), Bernie Leighton (Piano Player).

New York Stories: Oedipus Wrecks (1989)
Written and Directed by Woody Allen. Photography: Sven Nykvist. Editor:

Susan E. Morse. Costume Designer: Jeffrey Kurland. Production Designer: Santo Loquasto. Executive Producers: Jack Rollins, Charles H. Joffe. Produced by Robert Greenhut. A Jack Rollins-Charles H. Joffe Production. Released by Touchstone Pictures. Woody Allen (Sheldon), Mae Questel (mother), Mia Farrow (Lisa), Julie Kavner (Treva), Marvin Chatinover (psychiatrist), Jessie Keosian (Aunt Ceil).

Crimes and Misdemeanors (1989)
Written and Directed by Woody Allen. Photography: Sven Nykvist. Editor: Susan E. Morse. Costume Designer: Jeffrey Kurland. Production Designer: Santo Loquasto. Produced by Jack Rollins and Charles H. Joffe. Released by Orion Pictures. 104 minutes. Martin Landau (Judah Rosenthal), Claire Bloom (Miriam Rosenthal), Woody Allen (Clifford Stern), Mia Farrow (Halley Reed), Alan Alda (Lester), Sam Waterston (Ben), Anjelica Huston (Dolores Paley).

The Plays of Woody Allen

Don't Drink the Water!
Directed by Stanley Prager. Produced by David Merrick in association with Jack Rollins and Charles Joffe. Opened at the Morosco Theatre, New York City, November 17, 1966.
Original Cast

Father Drobney	Richard Libertini
Ambassador Magee	House Jameson
Kilroy	Gerry Matthews
Axel Magee	Tony Roberts
Marion Hollander	Kay Medford
Walter Hollander	Lou Jacobi
Susan Hollander	Anita Gillette
Krojack	James Kukas
Sultan of Bashir	Oliver Clark

Play It Again, Sam!
Presented by David Merrick in association with Jack Rollins and Charles Joffe. Opened at the Broadhurst Theatre, New York City, February 12, 1969.
Original Cast

Allan Felix	Woody Allen
Nancy	Sheila Sullivan
Humphrey Bogart	Jerry Lacey
Dick Christie	Tony Roberts
Linda Christie	Diane Keaton
Barbara	Barbara Brownell

The Floating Lightbulb
Directed by Ulu Grosbard. Produced by Richmond Crinkley for the Lincoln Center Theater Company. Opened at the Vivian Beaumont Theatre, New York City, April 27, 1981.
Original Cast

Paul Pollack	Brian Backer
Steve Pollack	Eric Gurry
Enid Pollack	Beatrice Arthur

Max Pollack	Danny Aiello
Betty	Ellen March
Jerry Wexler	Jack Weston

Books by Woody Allen

Fiction:
Getting Even. New York: Vintage Books, 1978.
Side Effects. New York: Random House, 1980.
Without Feathers. New York: Random House, 1975.

Plays:
Don't Drink the Water. New York: Samuel French, Inc., 1967.
The Floating Lightbulb. New York: Random House, 1982.
Play It Again, Sam! New York: Samuel French, Inc., 1969.

Screenplays:
Four Films of Woody Allen. New York: Random House, 1982.
Three Films of Woody Allen. New York: Random House, 1985.
Hannah and Her Sisters. New York: Vintage Books, 1986.

Records

Woody Allen: *The Nightclub Years.* United Artists. UA 9968, 1976.

Bibliography

Secondary Sources

Books

Adler, Bill, and Jeffrey Feinman. *Woody Allen, Clown Prince of American Humor.* New York: Pinnacle Books, 1975.

Aleichem, Sholom. *Old Country Tales.* New York: G. P. Putnam's Sons, 1966.

———. *Stories and Satires.* New York: Collier Books, 1959.

Bach, Steven. *Final Cut.* New York: William Morrow and Company, Inc., 1985.

Becker, Ernest. *The Denial of Death.* New York: The Free Press, 1973.

Boorstin, Daniel J. *The Image: A Guide to Pseudo-Events in America.* New York: Harper & Row Publishers, 1961.

Brode, Douglas. *Woody Allen, his films and career (sic).* Secaucus, New Jersey: Citadel Press, 1985.

Cervantes, Miguel de. *Don Quixote.* Middlesex: Penguin Classics, 1964.

Chaplin, Charles. *My Autobiography.* London: The Bodley Head Ltd., 1984.

Cohen, John, ed. *The Essential Lenny Bruce.* London: Papermac, 1987.

Dooley, Roger. *From Scarface to Scarlett.* New York: Harcourt Brace Jovanovich, 1981.

Fitzgerald, F. Scott. *The Great Gatsby.* Middlesex: Penguin Books, 1976.

Flashner, Graham. *Everything You Always Wanted to Know About Woody.* London: Robson Books Ltd., 1989.

Gershwin, Ira. *Lyrics on Several Occasions.* London: Elm Tree Books, 1977.

Guthrie, Lee. *Woody Allen, A Biography.* New York: Drake Publishers, 1978.

Hellman, Lillian. *Scoundrel Time.* London: Quartet Books, 1979.

Herman, Gary, comp. *The Book of Hollywood Quotes.* Menasha: Omnibus Press, 1979.

Hirsch, Foster. *Love, Sex, Death, and the Meaning of Life: Woody Allen.* New York: McGraw-Hill Paperbacks, 1981.

Howe, Irving. *World of Our Fathers.* New York: Bantam Books, 1980.

———, and Elizzer Greenberg. *A Treasure of Yiddish Stories.* New York: Holt, Rinehart and Winston, 1953.

Jacobs, Diane. *. . . but we need the eggs (sic).* New York: St. Martin's Press, 1983.

Kael, Pauline. *State of the Art.* New York: E. P. Dutton, 1985.

Kanin, Garson. *Together Again.* New York: Doubleday & Co., 1981.

Lasch, Christopher. *The Culture of Narcissism.* New York: Norton, 1979.

Lax, Eric. *Woody Allen and His Comedy.* London: Elm Tree Books, 1975.

Levine, Paul. *E. L. Doctorow*. London: Methuen, 1985.

McCann, Graham. *Woody Allen*. London: Polity Press, 1990.

McKnight, Gerald. *Joking Aside*. London: Star, 1983.

Maltin, Leonard. *The Great Movie Comedians*. New York: Crown, 1978.

Mann, Thomas. *Death in Venice*. New York: Vintage Books, 1936.

Mast, Gerald. *The Comic Mind*. The University of Chicago Press, 1979.

Miller, Edwin. *Seventeen Interviews: Filmstars and Superstars*. Rose Hill Triangle Publications, 1970.

Monaco, James. *American Film Now*. New York: New York Zoetrope, 1984.

Navacelle, Thierry de. *Woody Allen on Location*. London: Sidgwick and Jackson, 1987.

Navasky, Victor S. *Naming Names*. New York: The Viking Press, 1980.

Odets, Clifford. *Six Plays*. London: Methuen, 1982.

Palmer, Myles. *Woody Allen*. New York: Proteus, 1980.

Parish, James Robert, and William T. Leonard. *The Funsters*. Westport: Arlington House, 1979.

Patrick, John. *Teahouse of the August Moon*. London: William Heineman Ltd., 1955.

Pells, Richard H. *The Liberal Mind in a Conservative Age: American Intellectuals in the 1940s & 1950s*. New York: Harper and Row, 1985.

Perelman, S. J. *The Most of S. J. Perelman*. Eyre Methuen, 1978.

Probst, Leonard. *Off Camera*. New York: Stein and Day, 1975.

Rilke, Rainer Maria. *Selected Poems*. New York: Methuen, 1986.

Rosenblum, Ralph, and Robert Karen. *When the Shooting Stops . . . the Cutting Begins*. New York: The Viking Press, 1979.

Rosten, Leo. *The Joys of Yiddish*. Middlesex: Penguin Books, 1968.

Roth, Philip. *The Ghost Writer*. New York: Farrar, Strauss and Giroux, 1979.

———. *Goodbye, Columbus*. New York: Bantam Books, 1982.

———. *Portnoy's Complaint*. New York: Random House, 1969.

Runyon, Damon. *More Guys and Dolls*. Garden City Books, 1951.

Schickel, Richard. *Intimate Strangers: The Culture of Celebrity*. New York: Doubleday & Company, 1985.

Sinyard, Neil. *The Films of Woody Allen*. Leicester: Magna Books, 1988.

Sypher, Wylie, ed. *Comedy*. Baltimore: The Johns Hopkins University Press, 1980.

Tolstoy, Leo. *Anna Karenina*. Middlesex: Penguin Classics, 1978.

Tyler, Anne. *The Accidental Tourist*. Middlesex: Penguin Books, 1986.

Warshow, Robert. *The Immediate Experience*. New York: Atheneum, 1979.

Wilde, Larry. *The Great Movie Comedians Talk about Themselves*. Secaucus, N.J.: The Citadel Press, 1968.

Wisse, Ruth. *The Schlemiel as Modern Hero*. The University of Chicago Press, 1971.

Wolf, William. *Landmark Films*. New York: Paddington Press Ltd., 1979.

Yacowar, Maurice. *Loser Take All*. New York: Frederick Ungar Publishing Co., 1979.

BROOKLYN IS NOT EXPANDING

Articles

Arnold, Gary. "A Midsummer Night's Woody Allen." *International Herald Tribune* (July 26, 1982): 14.

Bennetts, Leslie. "Woody Allen's Selective Vision of New York." *New York Times* (March 7, 1986): C28.

Bizio, Silvio. "The Importance of Being Woody." *Empire* 14 (August 1990): 46–51.

Brown, Georgia A. "Much Ado about Mia." *American Film* xii: 5 (March 1987): 24–28.

Canby, Vincent. "Woody Allen Continues to Refine His Cinematic Art." *New York Times* (July 15, 1983): 1, 15.

———. " 'Zelig,' Woody Allen's Story about a 'Chameleon Man.' " *New York Times* (July 15, 1983): C8.

Corliss, Richard. "A Little Faith in People." *Film Comment* 15: 3 (May–June, 1979): 16–17.

———. "Pastrami and Tongue on Wry." *Time* 123 (January 23, 1984): 33.

———. "Retro-Romance in a Swanky Town." *Time* 127 (February 3, 1986): 43.

Dempsey, M. "The Autobiography of Woody Allen." *Film Comment* 15: 3 (May–June, 1979): 9–16.

Denby, David. "Love among the Little People." *New York Magazine* 18 (March 11, 1985): 97–98.

Didion, Joan. "Letter from Manhattan." *New York Review of Books* 26 (August 16, 1979): 18–19.

Drew, Bernard. "Woody Allen Is Feeling Better." *American Film* II: 7 (May 1977): 10–15.

Goldman, Steven. "A Liar, a Cheat and a Murderer." *Empire* 14 (August 1990): 51.

James, Caryn. "Auteur! Auteur!" *New York Times Magazine* (January 19, 1986): 18–30.

Kael, Pauline. "The Current Cinema." *The New Yorker* 61 (March 25, 1985): 104–9.

Kakutani, Michiko. "Books of the Times." *New York Times* (October 19, 1983).

———. "Feisty Mia Farrow." *International Herald Tribune* (January 28/29, 1984).

Karman, Mal. "Interviews with Woody Allen." *Milimeter* 5 (October 1977): 16–22.

Katsahnias, Iannis. "Gagnants et perdants." *Cahiers du Cinéma* 428 (February 1990): 20–21.

Kroll, Jack. "Funny, but He's Serious." *Newsweek* 91 (April 24, 1978): 42–49.

———. "The Heartbreak Kid." *Newsweek* 97 (May 11, 1981): 55.

———, with Katrine Ames and Janet Huck. "Thoroughly Modern Diane." *Newsweek* 99 (February 15, 1982): 43–46.

Lax, Eric. "Woody Allen—Not Only a Comic." *New York Times* (February 24, 1985): 1, 24.

Maltin, Leonard. "Take Woody Allen. Please!" *Film Comment* 10: 2 (March–April, 1974): 42–45.

Remnick, David. "Comedy isn't funny" *(sic)*. *Saturday Review* 12 (June 1986): 30–34.

Rosen, Nick. "Hurricane Woody hits town" *(sic)*. *Sunday Times.* (London) (May 6, 1984).

Rosenbaum, Ron. "The Fall and Rise of Barbara Hershey." *American Film* XI: 7 (May 1986): 20–25.

Saada, Nicolas. "Les Gammes de Woody Allen." *Cahiers du Cinéma* 428 (February 1990): 25.

Sarris, Andrew. "Woody Allen at the Peak of Parody." *Village Voice* (July 10, 1983): 39.

Schickel, Richard. "Woody Allen's Breakthrough Movie." *Time* 109 (April 25, 1977): 18–19.

———. "Meditations on Celebrity." *Time* 122 (July 11, 1983): 40.

———. "Woody Allen Comes of Age." *Time* 113 (April 30, 1979): 38–42.

Sinyard, Neil. "Woody Allen: Everyone's Favourite Failure." *Photoplay* 37: 7 (July 1986): 14–19.

Siskel, Gene. "Woody Allen on Love, Films, and Reagan." *Chicago Tribune* (July 11, 1982): 5–6.

Smith, Monty. "The Films of Woody Allen." *Empire* 14 (August 1990): 48–49.

Strauss, Frédéric. "Le Crime parfait." *Cahiers du Cinéma* 428 (February 1990): 22–23.

Wernblad, Annette. "The Purple Rose of Cairo." *Kosmorama* 173 (1985): 131–134.

———. "Radio Days." *Kosmorama* 181 (1987): 36.

Wetzsteon, Ross. "Woody Allen: Schlemiel as Sex Maniac." *Ms* 6 (November 1977): 14–15.

Young, Vernon. "Autumn Interiors." *Commentary* 67 (January 1979): 60–64.

"Love, Death and La-De-Dah." *Time* 110 (September 26, 1977): 40–45. [No byline]

Television

"To Woody Allen from Europe with Love" (Interview, shown on Danish TV on January 5, 1982).

Index